高等学校电子商务专业规划教材

国际商务函电写作与实训

姜少婷　唐付丽　孙桂兰　主编

清华大学出版社
北　京

内 容 简 介

随着外贸业务的持续增长,我国对外贸人才的要求也越来越高,这就需要学生掌握国际商务函电的特点和写作技能,提高他们将来在国际商务活动中运用英语的能力。同时,近年来国际外贸环境和跨国沟通交流方式都发生了变化,使得国际主流电子邮件的写法和思维架构也随之改变。基于此,本书以全新外贸思维模式为指导,从我国外贸业务的实际出发,借鉴国内外国际商务函电的结构与体系,梳理百余种外贸业务情景,详细介绍了国际商务函电的格式与结构、写作步骤、常用词语和表达方式等,通过大量的案例和实例,分享地道、简洁、与时俱进的电子邮件内容和写作手法。

本书按照外贸业务发展过程,共分8个单元,包括建立业务关系、询价及回复、报价与还价、付款方式、订单与确认、保险、装运、索赔与处理。每个单元主要包括背景知识介绍、写作步骤、必备词汇和句型、范例、讲解和实训题目。本书体现国际商务函电在实际外贸业务成交中所起到的作用,凸显教学改革的成果和先进的教育、教学理念。

本书力求贴近专业、贴近实践、实例驱动、应用为主,适合外经贸从业者和相关专业学生使用,也可供外贸专业教学研究者参考,不但能够帮助读者学会国际商务函电的写作,提升函电写作水平,更重要的是能够培养外贸从业者实用、高效的外贸谈判思维模式。

本书封面贴有清华大学出版社防伪标签,无标签者不得销售。
版权所有,侵权必究。举报: 010-62782989, beiqinquan@tup.tsinghua.edu.cn。

图书在版编目(CIP)数据

国际商务函电写作与实训/姜少婷,唐付丽,孙桂兰主编. —北京:清华大学出版社,2020.6(2023.1重印)
高等学校电子商务专业规划教材
ISBN 978-7-302-54834-8

Ⅰ.①国… Ⅱ.①姜… ②唐… ③孙… Ⅲ.①国际贸易-英语-电报信函-写作-高等学校-教材 Ⅳ.①F740

中国版本图书馆 CIP 数据核字(2020)第 021417 号

责任编辑:白立军　杨　帆
封面设计:常雪影
责任校对:李建庄
责任印制:朱雨萌

出版发行:清华大学出版社
网　　址: http://www.tup.com.cn, http://www.wqbook.com
地　　址:北京清华大学学研大厦 A 座　　　邮　编:100084
社 总 机: 010-83470000　　　邮　购: 010-62786544
投稿与读者服务: 010-62776969, c-service@tup.tsinghua.edu.cn
质量反馈: 010-62772015, zhiliang@tup.tsinghua.edu.cn
课件下载: http://www.tup.com.cn, 010-83470236

印 装 者:大厂回族自治县彩虹印刷有限公司
经　　销:全国新华书店
开　　本: 185mm×260mm　　　印　张: 6.5　　　字　数: 157 千字
版　　次: 2020 年 6 月第 1 版　　　印　次: 2023 年 1 月第 3 次印刷
定　　价: 29.80 元

产品编号: 070329-01

FOREWORD

前言

目前，国家对高素质的外贸类人才的需求日益增加，因此也对高等院校外贸英语类高素质人才培养目标提出了新的要求。有鉴于此，清华大学出版社组织启动了"外贸英语"专业教材的编写和出版工作。本书正是为了适应当今时代对高层次外贸类人才培养的需求而编写的。

《国际商务函电写作与实训》在商务英语专业、国际贸易专业和国际商务专业人才培养过程中占有重要的地位，能够使学生掌握国际商务函电的基本理论、基本知识和基本技能，并初步具有国际商务函电写作的能力。在培养高效商务英语人才的全局中，具有增加学生对涉外商务工作的适应能力和开发创新能力的作用。本书旨在使读者掌握国际商务函电的基本知识、专业术语及表达方法，让读者熟悉对外贸易业务各个环节，锻炼其对相关业务的英语表达能力，并掌握涉外经贸工作中国际商务函电的写作技巧，以适应外经贸工作的实际业务需要。通过学习本书，希望读者在国际商务函电知识、读写能力等方面达到一定水平。

本书以适应社会需求为目标，以应用型能力培养为主线组织编写，在内容上按照知识的连贯性兼顾"实用"的原则进行取舍，主要体现出如下特色。

(1) 本书是应用型教材，定位准确，目标明确，以对外经贸商务活动的成交过程为主线，逐步展开，条理清晰，遵循了外贸常规流程。每章安排了背景介绍、写作模块等内容，有利于课堂教学和自学，使读者清楚每章应掌握的具体能力。

(2) 每章都附带专业性和实用性非常强的外贸英语词汇、句型和格式，同时对很多单词配有音标和例句讲解，方便记忆和背诵，系统强化了对外贸业务活动中各种商务英语函电的格式与结构、写作特点、专业术语、相关句型和常见表达方式等的掌握。课后实训部分能让读者及时巩固所学知识，并且最后一题都是与该章匹配的写作练习，能让读者掌握并牢固写作能力。

(3) 顺应新时代背景下外贸发展趋势及国际商务函电的书写习惯，在充分研究国外客户外贸交际用语的基础上精选出国际贸易活动的最新材料和外贸实例，具有很强的实用性，在学生将来踏入职场、面对实际业务操作中可以作为随时的参考，且有效培养了学生举一反三的能力。

FOREWORD

（4）将国际商务函电的写作和外贸英语谈判实际技巧巧妙结合，例如在 Unit 3 中卖方回复买方的还价邮件中，通过要求买方用增加购买量而给予一定优惠的方式，既成功地拒绝了买方的还价，又增加了买方的购买量，并通过优惠的价格吸引对方达成合同。

（5）尤其注重精练、简洁，所有常用句型、词语和范例全部采用目前外贸行业较为常用的惯用语言，讲解通俗易懂且清楚到位。

本书主要包括 8 个单元：首先介绍买卖双方如何通过函电建立业务关系(Unit 1)；其次是买方询价(Unit 2)和卖方给出报价(Unit 3)；再次，双方共同商定付款方式(Unit 4)并确认订单(Unit 5)；最后是办理保险(Unit 6)、完成装运(Unit 7)和索赔与处理(Unit 8)。

本书由姜少婷、唐付丽、孙桂兰主编，全书共 8 个单元，其中姜少婷编写了 Unit 1、Unit 2、Unit 4、Unit 7，唐付丽编写了 Unit 3、Unit 5、Unit 6，孙桂兰编写了 Unit 8。

希望本书能有助于培养适应中国特色社会主义发展需要的、素质全面的新型外贸人才。相信本书能达到这个目标，且从形式到内容都成为精品，为教师和学生及专业人士所喜爱。

由于编者水平有限，书中难免有不妥和错误之处，恳请广大读者及同行专家批评指正，以便于再版修订完善。

编　者

2020 年 4 月

目 录

Unit 1　建立业务关系
　　　　（**Establishing Business Relations**）　　1
　Part 1　定义及写作步骤　　2
　Part 2　范例及讲解　　6
　Part 3　实训　　9

Unit 2　询价及回复
　　　　（**Inquiry & Reply**）　　12
　Part 1　定义及写作步骤　　13
　Part 2　范例及讲解　　16
　Part 3　实训　　22

Unit 3　报价与还价
　　　　（**Offer and Counter-offer**）　　25
　Part 1　定义及写作步骤　　26
　Part 2　范例及讲解　　29
　Part 3　实训　　36

Unit 4　付款方式
　　　　（**Payment Method**）　　38
　Part 1　定义及写作步骤　　39
　Part 2　范例及讲解　　42
　Part 3　实训　　47

Unit 5　订单与确认
　　　　（**Orders and Acknowledgment**）　　50
　Part 1　定义及写作步骤　　51
　Part 2　范例及讲解　　55
　Part 3　实训　　59

CONTENTS

Unit 6　保险
　　　　（**Insurance**） 61
　　Part 1　定义及写作步骤 62
　　Part 2　范例及讲解 65
　　Part 3　实训 68

Unit 7　装运
　　　　（**Shipment**） 72
　　Part 1　定义及写作步骤 73
　　Part 2　范例及讲解 76
　　Part 3　实训 82

Unit 8　索赔与处理
　　　　（**Claims and Settlement**） 84
　　Part 1　定义及写作步骤 85
　　Part 2　范例及讲解 88
　　Part 3　实训 94

参考文献 97

Unit 1

建立业务关系
（Establishing Business Relations）

国际商务函电主要包括信函、电报、传真及 E-mail 等形式,用于有效传递外贸业务信息。由于当前外贸业务最主要是以 E-mail 来沟通的,因此本教材的范文及样例主要采用 E-mail 的格式。一封合格的函电应该遵循 3C 原则,即清楚(clarity)、简洁(conciseness)和礼貌(courtesy)。

Part 1　定义及写作步骤

1. 定义

建立业务关系,实际就是确定贸易对象。一笔贸易通常始于卖方向潜在客户发送建立业务关系的邮件。

没有顾客就没有贸易,贸易对象选择是否合适决定着贸易的成败。通常,双方通过互相或第三方的介绍,先确认对方的资金信用、经营能力和业务范围等重要条件,然后才进行实质性的磋商。贸易双方只有相互了解、彼此信赖,才能顺利实现合作。

2. 写作步骤

(1)信息来源(source of information)。通过什么渠道得到对方的姓名、地址,例如:ads on the website(网站上的广告)、information on the Internet(网络上的信息)、contact at the exhibition(展览会上的接触)、company that both parties know(双方认识的公司)。

情景搭配用语:

- We have obtained your E-mail address from the website of…
  我们从……网站上得知您的邮箱。
- ××× has recommended/introduced you to us.
  ×××把贵公司介绍给了我们。
- Glad to find your E-mail address from…
  很高兴从……得到贵公司的邮箱。
- We learn through/from…that…
  我们通过……得知……
- On the recommendation of…
  由……介绍

例句:

- We have obtained your E-mail address from the website of www.××××.com.
- Mr. Jones, your trade partner in Beijing, has recommended you to us as a leading importer in Korea of lightweight batteries for vehicles.
- Glad to find your E-mail address from the website of www.××××.com.

(2)写信目的(intention of writing letter)。想与对方做什么生意,如推荐自己的产品。

情景搭配用语:

- We are willing to…
  我们愿意……

- We express our desire to…
  我们希望……
- We are writing to you for the…
  我们现写信愿意……
- We are desirous of…
  我们愿意……

例句：
- We are willing to enter into business relations with you.
- We express our desire to enter into business relationship with you.
- In order to expand the sales of our products into America, we are writing to you for cooperation possibilities.
- We are desirous of establishing long-term trade relations with you.

（3）自我介绍（self-introduction）。自我介绍包括公司介绍和产品介绍。其中，公司介绍包括公司性质、业务范围、优势等，如经验丰富、供货渠道稳定、销售广泛等；产品介绍包括价格、质量、销量等，还可以另附目录、报价单或寄样品供对方参考。

情景搭配用语：
- We wish to introduce ourselves to you as a…
  我们愿向贵方介绍，我们是一家……
- Our lines are mainly…
  我们主要从事……
- …fall within the scope of our business activities.
  ……属于我们的经营范围。

例句：
- We wish to introduce ourselves to you as a state-operated corporation dealing exclusively in light industrial products.
- Our lines are mainly textiles and handicrafts.
- Electronic products fall within the scope of our business activities.

（4）期望（expectation）。表达与对方合作和早日收到回复的愿望。

情景搭配用语：
- We look forward to receiving…
  我们希望早日收到……
- Hope to receive …
  希望收到……
- …will be really appreciated.
  ……会非常感激。
- We are anticipating your answer.
  我们盼望您尽快回复。

例句：

UNIT 1

- We are looking forward to your specific inquiry.
- Your comments on our products or any information on your markets demand will be really appreciated.

必备词汇和句型

1. recommendation [ˌrekəmenˈdeɪʃən] *n.* 推荐,介绍
2. inform *v.* 通知
3. enter into business relations 建立业务关系
4. catalogue [ˈkætəlɒg] *n.* 目录
5. for your reference 供您参考
6. launch *v.* 发布,开发
   a newly launched product 一个新开发的产品
7. promptly [ˈprɒmptlɪ] *adv.* 立即
8. representative [ˌreprɪˈzentətɪv] *n.* 代表
9. chamber [ˈtʃeɪmbə(r)] of commerce [ˈkɒmɜːs] 商会
10. specialize [ˈspeʃəlaɪz] *v.* 专门经营,擅长
    specialize in 专门经营
11. on the bases [ˈbeɪsiːs] of equality [ɪˈkwɒlətɪ] and mutual [ˈmjuːtʃʊəl] benefit 在平等互利的基础上
12. pamphlet [ˈpæmflɪt] *n.* 小册子   pamphlet = booklet [ˈbʊklɪt]
    They issued a pamphlet concerning [kənˈsɜːnɪŋ] their newly launched products.
    他们出了一本有关新开发产品的小册子。
13. a range [reɪndʒ] of 一套,一系列
    The slim booklets describe a range of services and facilities.
    这些薄薄的小册子介绍了一系列服务和设施。
14. make offers 报价
15. import [ˈɪmpɔːt] and export [ˈekspɔːt] corporation 进出口公司
16. silk *n.* 丝绸
17. cotton piece goods 棉布
18. blouse [blaʊz] *n.* 女衬衫
19. be of the latest style 最新式样
20. financial [faɪˈnænʃl] position 财务状况
21. trade reputation 贸易声誉
22. on display 展出
23. woolen [ˈwʊlɪn] knitwear [ˈnɪtweə(r)] 毛织品
24. garment [ˈɡɑːmənt] *n.* 服装
25. meet with great favor 受欢迎

26. credit standing 信用地位,商业信誉
27. state-operated ['ɒpəreɪtɪd] 国营的
28. currency ['kʌrənsi] n. 货币
    Chinese currency 中国货币
    British currency 英国货币
29. investment n. 投资
    investor 投资者
    direct investment 直接投资
    a profitable ['prɒfɪtəbl] investment 有利可得的投资
    a long-term investment 长期投资
    investment intent [ɪn'tent] 投资意向
    investment partner 投资伙伴
    investment environment [ɪn'vaɪrənmənt] 投资环境
30. enterprise n. 企业,公司,事业
    joint venture ['ventʃə(r)] enterprise 合资企业
    cooperative [kəʊ'ɒpərətɪv] enterprise 合作企业
    state-owned enterprise 国有企业
    exclusively foreign-owned enterprise 外商独资企业
    collectively-owned enterprise 集体企业
    individually [ˌɪndɪ'vɪdʒuəli] owned enterprise 个体企业
31. item n. 商品,项目
    item、goods、freight、merchandise、commodity 这些名词都可表示"商品、货物"之意。
    goods 货物   goods = freight
    merchandise 很正式的词,泛指商品,不特指某一商品
    commodity 主要指商场卖品或日用品
    daily commodity 日用品,必需品
    marketable commodity 易销品,适销品
    shortage of commodity 物资缺乏,短缺商品
32. enjoy a good reputation 享有盛誉
    enjoy a good reputation = enjoy great popularity
    类似的表达方法如下:
    The goods are most popular with our customers.
    The goods are universally acknowledged/acclaimed by our customers.
    The goods enjoy fast sales.
33. light industrial products 轻工业产品
    分类如下:
    textile 纺织品,包括天然纤维(cotton, silk clothing)和合成纤维(nylon, polyester clothing)

> foodstuff 食品
> cereal ['sɪərɪəl] 谷物
> cosmetics 化妆品
> chemicals 化学药品
> electrical goods 电器产品(fridge, TV, washing machine)
> hardware 五金制品
> arts & crafts 工艺品

34. We shall be appreciative/grateful/ thankful/ obliged if…
    如能……我们将不胜感激。
35. favorable *adj.* 有利的,赞成的,有帮助的,优惠的
    favorable offer   优惠报价
    favorable reply   佳音,回复

Part 2   范例及讲解

1. 建立业务关系(开发客户)

To: Kevin Green
From: Aaron Liu
Subject: Fishing net supplier

Dear Mr. Green,

　　We **obtain**① your E-mail address from the website of www.××××.com, and glad to know that you are **in the market for**② fishing net.(信息来源)

　　We are factory **specializing in**③ the manufacture and **export**④ of fishing net for more than 7 years, supplying all kinds of high-quality fishing nets with **competitive price**⑤. We **enclosed**⑥ a copy of our export list **covering**⑦ the hot-selling items **suppliable**⑧ at present.(自我介绍)

　　We are desirous of establishing long-term trade relations with you. Should any of these items **be of interest to you**⑨, we will be happy to give you details.(写信的目的及愿望)

Yours faithfully,
Aaron Liu

【讲解】
① obtain   *v.* 获得,取得   obtain = get

We obtain/get your E-mail from Legenda Company.

我们从 Legenda 公司获得了贵方的邮箱。

Now a lot of information can be obtained from the Internet.

现在可以从因特网获得许多的信息。

② in the market for　需要……,有意购买

③ specialize in　专门经营,擅长

We specialize in power saws and drills.

我们专门经营电锯和电钻。

④ export　*v.& n.* 出口　　反义词：import　*v.& n.* 进口

We export a large quantity of bicycles now.

我们现在出口大量的自行车。

We are interested in the import of bicycles.

我们对进口自行车感兴趣。

⑤ competitive price　有竞争力的价格(即较低的价格)

Our prices are competitive.

我们的价格有竞争力。

⑥ enclose　*v.* 随函附上,附录是　We enclose＝Attached are/is

We enclose some photos of our showroom(＝Attached are some photos of our showroom)。

附录是我们样品间的一些展示图片。

⑦ cover　*v.* 包含

The survey covers all aspects of the business.

调查包括这家企业的各个方面。

⑧ suppliable　*adj.* 可提供的

Please make us the most favorable offer, stating origin, packing, quantity suppliable and the earliest time of shipment.

请报最优惠的价格,注明原产地区、包装、供货数量和最早装运日期。

⑨ sth. be of interest to you　您对……感兴趣

Should any of these items be of interest to you(＝if you are interested in any of these items)。

如果您对任何一款产品感兴趣。

【译文】

亲爱的格林先生：

　　我们从 www.××××.com 上获得了您的电子邮件地址,得知您正在购买渔网。我们工厂专业从事渔网生产和出口已经 7 年多了,提供各种高品质的渔网,价格非常有竞争力。随函附上我方出口产品的目录,包括目前可以供应的热销产品。我们希望与你方建立长期的贸易关系。如果您对任何一款产品感兴趣,我们将很

UNIT 1

> 高兴为您提供产品的详细信息。
>
> 刘亚伦谨上

备注：Kevin Green 这个名字中，Kevin 是名，Green 是姓。可以用 Dear Kevin（更亲切），或者 Dear Mr. Green（更正式）。

2. 介绍自己的优势

> To：Kevin Green
> From：Aaron Liu
> Subject：Advantages
>
> Dear Mr. Green，
>
>   I have enclosed **the 3rd party**[①] testing report. We **feel sure**[②] that our fishing nets could meet your quality level.
>
>   Please kindly also **find**[③] our advantages below.
>
>   (1) Specialized in manufacturing fishing net for over 7 years.
>
>   (2) **The source of production**[④] with competitive price.
>
>   (3) Experienced in **cooperating with**[⑤] importers in your country.
>
>   (4) **Customization acceptable**[⑥].
>
>   (5) **Quick and safe delivery**[⑦].
>
>   (6) **Free samples**[⑧] suppliable.
>
>   (7) Free samples can be sent **on request**[⑨].
>
>   Call me, let's talk more!
>
> Yours faithfully,
> Aaron Liu
> Cell Phone：86133××××××××

【讲解】

① the 3rd party   第三方

② feel sure   确信 feel sure = have full of confidence

③ find   v.查看，看看 find = see

④ the source of production   工厂源头生产（没有中间商赚差价）

⑤ cooperate with   与……合作

⑥ customization acceptable   可接受定制

customization   *n.* 定制

acceptable   *adj.* 可以接受的

⑦ quick and safe delivery   快速、安全地送达

⑧ free samples   免费样品

⑨ on request   按(您的)要求

【译文】

> 亲爱的格林先生：
>
> 　　我随函附上第三方的测试报告。我们确信我们的渔网可以满足您的质量水平。
>
> 　　另外请允许我介绍一下我们的优势。
>
> （1）专业生产渔网7年以上。
>
> （2）源头厂家，价格有优势。
>
> （3）有与贵国进口商合作的经验。
>
> （4）可接受定制。
>
> （5）快速、安全交货。
>
> （6）免费样品供应。
>
> （7）随时可按要求为您寄出免费样品。
>
> 请打电话给我，我们再聊吧！
>
> 刘亚伦谨上
手机：86133×××××××

Part 3　实训

1. Translate the following sentences into Chinese.

（1）We are a state-operated corporation, handling the export of garments and we are willing to enter into business relations with your firm.

（2）This is to introduce the Pacific Corporation as exporters of light industrial products having business relations with more than 80 countries in the world.

（3）We write to introduce ourselves as exporter of fresh water pearls having many years' experience in this particular line of business.

（4）We take the opportunity to introduce ourselves as large importers of fertilizers in our country.

（5）On the recommendation of Harvey Co., we have learned with pleasure the name of your firm.

UNIT 1

（6）We express our desire to establish business relations with your firm.

（7）We shall be glad to enter into business relations with you.

2. Translate the following sentences into English.

（1）我们现在借此机会致函贵公司，希望与贵公司建立业务关系。

（2）我们专营中国食品的出口业务，希望在这一行业与贵公司合作。

（3）我们的互相理解和合作一定会带来重要的业务。

（4）我们获知贵公司经营轻工产品，想和贵公司建立业务关系。

（5）我们的产品以高品质、时尚的设计和具有竞争力的价格享誉国内外。

（6）我们对进出口化学制品感兴趣。

（7）如果你方能尽早报价我们将非常感谢。

3. Write a letter of establishing business relations.

现在假设你是青岛一家外贸公司的外贸专员林佳音，从 www.××××.com 网站得知澳大利亚悉尼的 PEDSON 公司想要购买山地车，并想在中国内地寻求长期合作关系的客户。

请给该公司的负责人 Martin White 女士写一封想与之建立业务关系的邮件。

【答案】

1. Translate the following sentences into Chinese.

（1）我们是一家国有企业，经营服装出口，希望和贵公司建立业务关系。

（2）现介绍太平洋公司，它是轻工产品的出口商，与世界上80多个国家都有业务关系。

（3）作为有多年出口经验的淡水珍珠出口商，我们写信介绍自己。

（4）作为我国大型的化肥进口商，我们借此机会介绍自己。

（5）通过哈维公司的介绍，我们得知了贵公司的名字。

（6）我们希望与贵公司建立业务关系。

（7）我们很高兴与贵公司建立业务关系。

2. Translate the following sentences into English.

（1）We now avail ourselves of this opportunity to write to you with a view to entering into business relations with you.

（2）Specializing in the export of Chinese foodstuffs, we wish to express our desire to trade with you in this line.

（3）Our mutual understanding and cooperation will certainly result in important business.

（4）We have learned that your firm specializes in Light Industrial Goods, and we are willing to establish business relationship with you.

（5）Our products enjoyed a high popularity internationally for their high quality, fashionable design and competitive price.

（6）We are interested in the import and export of chemicals.

（7）We shall be very grateful if you can make us an offer early.

3. Write a letter of establishing business relations.

Dear Ms. White,

　　We obtain your E-mail address from the website of www.××××.com, and glad to know that you are in the market for mountain bike.

　　We are willing to enter into business relations with you. Specializing in the export of mountain bike with more than 10 years, we enjoy a high popularity internationally for their high quality, fashionable design and competitive price. We enclose a catalogue and a price list.

　　We are looking forward to your early reply.

Yours faithfully,
Jiayin Lin

Unit 2

询价及回复
（Inquiry & Reply）

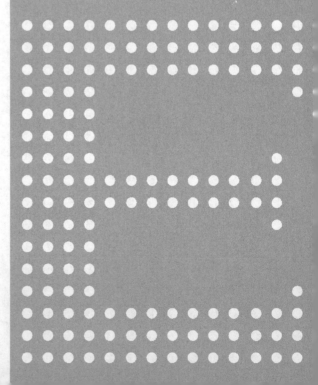

Part 1　定义及写作步骤

1. 定义

买方向卖方(或卖方向买方)询问某商品的交易条件(如价格、规格、品质、数量、包装、装运或索取样品等)。

注意：

(1) 询价又称为询盘(inquiry/enquiry)，通常由买方向卖方发出。询盘不是交易的必经程序，如彼此都已了解对方，可以忽略此步骤。

(2) 询价不具备法律上的约束力，双方对能否达成协议不负有任何责任，可以同时向若干个交易对象发出询价。

(3) 询价分为一般询价和具体询价。

一般询价(general inquiry)：索取一般资料，如目录(catalogue/catalog)、价目表或报价单(price list or quotation sheet)、样品(sample)、图片(illustrated photo prints)等。

具体询价(specific inquiry)：询问具体商品名称(the name of the commodity)、规格(the specifications)、数量(the quantity)、单价(the unit price)、装船期(the time of shipment)、付款条件(the terms of payment)等。

2. 写作步骤

(1) 信息来源和自我介绍。

- We learn from…that you are one of the leading manufacturers of…in China.
- We are one of the leading importers engaged in…
- We are an importer/exporter handling…for many years.

(2) 求购意向。

- We are considering the purchase of…
- We are interested in importing…
- We will place a large order with you for this product.

(3) 询问报价及有关交易条件。

- We appreciate your detailed information about the product as well as your competitive price.
- Please send us your catalogues and quotations.
- Please kindly provide the minimum order quantity and payment terms.
- We'll be pleased to have your catalogues and quotations.
- Please make us your best quotation for…

(4) 期望。

- We hope this will be a good start for a long and profitable business relations.
- If you can supply the goods at very competitive prices, we will place a large order with you.
- Looking forward to your early reply.

必备词汇和句型

1. inquire [ɪnˈkwaɪə] *v.* 询价   inquire = enquire
   inquire sth. 或 inquire about/for sth.   询问某事
   We are inquiring about the supply of sugar and coffee.
   我方正在询问购糖和咖啡的货源。

2. inquiry [ɪnˈkwaɪəri] *n.* 询价   inquiry = enquiry
   general inquiry   一般询盘
   specific inquiry   具体询盘
   make an inquiry for sth. = inquire for sth.   对某物询价
   keep the inquiry on file   把询价记录在案

3. dealer [ˈdiːlə] *n.* 商人

4. quote [kwəʊt] *v.* 报价   quotation [kwəʊˈteɪʃn] *n.* 报价

5. offer *v.& n.* 报价

6. sales department   销售部

7. sample [ˈsɑːmpəl] *n.* 样品

8. a long-term contract   长期合同

9. discount [ˈdɪskaʊnt] *n.* 折扣

10. grant [grɑːnt] *v.* 批准

11. process [ˈprəʊses] *v.* 加工

12. guarantee [ˌɡærənˈtiː] *v.* 保证   guarantor [ˌɡærənˈtɔː] *n.* 保证人

13. interest *n.* 兴趣   *v.* 使…感兴趣
    have /take/feel no interest in sth.   对某物不感兴趣
    be interested to do sth.   对做某事感兴趣
    We have /feel no interest in the terms of payment on a D/A basis.
    我们不想用承兑交单的付款方式。
    We are interested in the import of Chinese silk neckties.
    我们对进口中国丝绸领带感兴趣。
    They are interested to export Chinese silk scarves.
    他们对出口中国丝巾感兴趣。

14. market *n.* 市场,行市   *v.* 推销,销售
    They are in the market for table-cloths and pillowcases.
    他们要购买桌布和枕头套。
    The market is strengthening.
    行情在上涨。
    There is no difficulty in marketing these products in the Asian market.
    在亚洲市场推销这些产品不会有困难。

In order to meet your needs in marketing, we take this opportunity to recommend *Good Luck* Brand Electric Fans.

为满足你方的销售需求,我方借此机会向你方推荐"好运"牌电风扇。

15. place *v.* 订货

    If the quality of your goods is good and the price is acceptable to us, we will place a large order with you.

    如你方产品的质量好,价格可接受,我们将与你方大量订货。

    We regret that our customers have placed their orders elsewhere.

    很遗憾我方的客户在其他地方已经订货了。

16. order *n.* 订单

    place/make/send an order for sth.   订购某货物

    If your price is in line, we will send you an order for 1,000 sets.

    如果你方价格与市价相符,我方将订购1000台。

    Can you supply the goods from stock if we order immediately?

    如果我方立即订货,你方能有现货供应吗?

    If you allow us 5% discount, we will order 5,000 dozen.

    如果你方给予5%的折扣,我方将订购5000打。

17. competitor [kəmˈpetɪtə] *n.* 竞争对手

    The superior quality, attractive design and favorable price of their products will enable them to defeat the competitors.

    他们产品优良的质量,诱人的设计,合理的价格,将使他们击败竞争对手。

18. reference [ˈrefərəns] *n.* 谈及,参考

    A copy of our feasibility [ˌfiːzəˈbɪlətiː] study report will be sent to you for your reference.

    我们将寄送一份可行性研究报告供你方参考。

    with (in) reference to   关于

    With reference to our credit standing, please contact our banker for information.

    关于我方的信誉状况,请向我方银行咨询。

19. available *adj.* 可利用的,可供应的,可得到的(做定语时前置或后置均可,后置较为常用)

    commodities available for export   供出口的商品

    sth. is/are not available   缺货

    The only opportunity available now is the Harbin Fair.

    目前唯一的机会就是哈尔滨交易会。

    Attached is a catalog covering the goods available at present.

    随函附上一份我方目前可供货的目录单。

20. catalog [ˈkætəlɒg] = catalogue [ˈkætəlɒg] *n.* 目录

Part 2 范例及讲解

1. 一般询价及回复（General inquiry & reply）
范例 1：Buyer's inquiry

> To：Allen Chen
> From：Bert Smith
> Subject：Inquiry for machinery
>
> Dear Mr. Chen,
> 　　We learn from GLU Co. Ltd, New York that you are a leading exporter of machinery in China.（信息来源）
> 　　We are very much interested in importing your machinery goods.（求购意向）
> 　　Please send us a catalogue and price list or even some samples if possible. We appreciate your detailed information of **CIF**① Qingdao prices, **discounts**②, and **terms of payment**③.（询问报价及有关交易条件）
> 　　We hope this will be a good start for a long and **profitable**④ business relations.（期望）
>
> Yours faithfully,
> Bert Smith

【讲解】
① CIF 是一种价格术语　CIF＝Cost, Insurance and Freight（成本、运费和保险）
类似的术语还有 CFR＝Cost and Freight（成本和运费）；FOB＝Free on Board（成本）
② discount　*n.* 折扣
allow/give/grant (sb.)…% discount off/on the prices of goods
按货价给予……%的折扣
If you order for 5,000 sets, we would grant you a 10% discount.
如果你方能定购 5000 台，我们将给予 10%的折扣。
We give 10% discount for cash payment.
我们予以现金付款九折优待。
③ terms of payment 支付条件，是对支付的货币、金额、方式（汇付、托收、信用证）、支付时间的规定
④ profitable [ˈprɒfɪtəbl]　*adj.* 可获利的,有利的
profitable fields of investment　有利的投资场所
profit　*n.* 利润（常用复数）

net profits　净利润，纯利润
gross profits　毛利润
total profits　总利润
profit ratio（rate）　利润率
sell sth. at a profit　出售某货物而获利

【译文】

亲爱的陈先生：
　　我们从纽约 GLU 有限公司获悉，贵公司是中国领先的机械出口商。
　　我们非常有兴趣进口您的机械产品。
　　如果可能，请将目录和价目表或一些样品发送给我们。我们感谢您提供 CIF 青岛价格、折扣和付款条件的详细信息。
　　我们希望这将是一个长期盈利业务关系的良好开端。

伯特·史密斯谨上

范例 2：Seller's reply

To：Allen Chen
From：Bert Smith
Subject：Products catalog & price list

Dear Bert,
　　We welcome you for your enquiry of March 21 and thank you for your interest in our export **commodities**①.
　　We enclose some copies of our illustrated catalogs and a price list giving the details you asked for. We feel sure you will agree that our products **appeal**② to the most selective buyers.
　　We allow a proper discount according to the quantity ordered. As to the terms of payment, we usually require **L/C payable by sight draft**③.
　　We are looking forward to your order and please be **assured**④ that it will receive our prompt and careful attention.

Yours faithfully,
Allen Chen

UNIT 2

【讲解】

① commodity ［kəˈmɒdəti］ n. 商品,物资
commodity exchange 商品交易所
daily commodity 日用品,必需品

② appeal ［əˈpiːl］ v. 有吸引力,要求
appeal to… 对……有吸引力
appeal to the most selective buyer 吸引最挑剔的买主

③ L/C payable by sight draft 即期信用证
L/C(letter of credit) 信用证
payable = available 可得到的
sight draft 即期　　by sight draft = at sight
L/C payable by sight draft = L/C available at sight

④ assure ［əˈʃʊə］ v. 向……保证,使确信
assure sb. of sth.
We assure you of the reliability of the information.
我们可以向你方保证这条信息的可靠性。
assure sb. that
We assure you that we shall do our best to expedite shipment.
请确信我们将迅速装运。
be assured of sth.
Please be assured of our continued cooperation.
请相信我方仍将继续合作。
be assured that
Please be assured that we will contact you as soon as our fresh supply comes in.
一旦确信我方新货源已到,我方即与你方联系。

【译文】

> 亲爱的伯特:
> 　　我们欢迎您3月21日的询价,并感谢您对我们出口商品的兴趣。
> 　　我们附上一些图解目录的副本和一份价格表,列出您要求的详细信息。我们相信您会认同我们的产品能够征服最挑剔的买家。
> 　　我们根据订购的数量给予适当的折扣。关于付款方式,我们通常要求用即期信用证的方式。
> 　　我们期待着您的订单,请放心,我们会及时、仔细地处理。
>
> 　　　　　　　　　　　　　　　　　　　　　　　　　陈艾伦谨上

2. 具体询价(Specific inquiry)

范例1：**Buyer's inquiry**

> To：Angel Li
> From：Chris Brown
> Subject：Inquiry for Printed Shirting No.156
>
> Dear Ms.Li,
>   We are glad to note from your letter of March 9 that, as an exporter of Chinese Cotton Piece Goods, you **are desirous of**① entering into direct business relations with us. This happens to **coincide**② with our desire.（信息来源和自我介绍）
>   At present, we are interested in Printed Shirting No.156 and shall be pleased to receive your product catalogs, samples and all necessary information **regarding**③ these goods so as to acquaint us with the quality and workmanship of your supplies.（求购意向）
>   Meanwhile please **quote**④ us your lowest price, CIF Vancouver, **inclusive**⑤ of our 5% **commission**⑥, stating the earliest date of shipment.（询问报价及有关交易条件）
>   Should your price be found competitive, we intend to place a large order with you.（期望）
>
> Yours faithfully,
> Chris Brown

【讲解】

① be desirous of 渴望,想要
We are desirous of entering into (to enter into) direct business relations with you.
我们热切盼望与您建立直接的贸易关系。
desire [dɪˈzaɪə(r)] *n.& v.* 期望,请求(比 wish 强烈)
What do you desire to buy at present?
你们目前想要买些什么?
It is desired that the catalogs shall be sent to us within 2 days.
深盼在两天内给我们目录本。
② coincide [ˌkəʊɪnˈsaɪd] *v.* (意见等)一致,(时间上)相同
We are glad that our ideas coincide.
很高兴我们双方意见一致。
Your inquiry coincided with our offer.
你方询盘正好与我方报盘同时发出。

③ regarding *prep.* 关于　　与 with regard to, in regard to, as regards 同义

We have already written to you regarding this matter.

关于此事我们已给您写过信。

④ quote [kwəʊt] *v.* 报价

quote sb. a price for sth.　向某人报……的价格

Please quote us your lowest price for walnuts.

请向我方报核桃的最低价。

⑤ inclusive [ɪnˈkluːsɪv] *adj.* 包括的　　be inclusive of sth. = including sth.

This price is inclusive of your 2% commission (= This price includes your 2% commission).

此价格包括您2%的佣金。

⑥ commission [kəˈmɪʃn] *n.* 佣金,委员会,任命

佣金是买方给予卖方的货款中应支付给中间商的一部分。卖方在收到货款后,应向中间商支付佣金。国际贸易中的常用词语"含佣价"就是包含佣金的价格,称为含佣价,即

含佣价=净价/(1-佣金率)

佣金通常用字母 C 表示。如每公吨(1 公吨=1000 千克)1000 美元 CFR 西雅图包含佣金2%,可写成:每公吨 1000 美元 CFRC2%西雅图。其中,C2%表示佣金率为2%。

Please quote us your lowest price, CIF, Vancouver, inclusive of our 5% commission (= Please quote us your lowest price, CIF, Vancouver, including our 5% commission).

请向我方报 CIF 温哥华的最低价,包括我方 5%佣金。

【译文】

> 亲爱的李女士:
> 　　我们很高兴在您3月9日的来信中得知,作为中国棉花商品的出口商,您希望与我们建立直接的业务关系。这恰好与我们的愿望吻合。
> 　　目前,我们对156号印花衬衫感兴趣,并乐于收到你方的产品目录、样品和有关这些商品的所有必要信息,以便让我们了解您的产品质量和工艺。
> 　　同时请以最低价格向我们报价 CIF 温哥华,包括我们5%佣金,并说明最早的发货日期。
> 　　如果你方的价格具有竞争力,我们打算向你方下大订单。
>
> 　　　　　　　　　　　　　　　　　　　　　　　　　　　克里斯·布朗谨上

范例 2: Seller's reply

> From: Angel Li
> To: Chris Brown

Subject: Quotes for Printed Shirting No 156

Dear Chris,

  Very glad to receive your inquiry for our Printed Shirting No 156.

  I have **checked**① with our manager and the lowest price we could offer you is USD78 per **dozen**② CIF Vancouver, inclusive of your 5% commission. The earliest date of shipment would be May 12. Our offer **is subject to** ③ your **confirmation**④ before March 25.

  We enclose a quote sheet of Printed Shirting No.156 in detail **for your review**⑤. Samples could be prepared in 4 working days and please provide your address in detail.

  We look forward to your reply soon.

Yours faithfully,
Angel Li

【讲解】

① check   *v.* 核实,商量

You'd better check with Joshua what time he's expecting us tonight.

你最好向约书亚核实一下他今晚要见我们的时间。

② dozen   *n.* 一打(12 个)

Give me two dozen eggs.

给我来两打(24 个)鸡蛋。

③ be subject to   根据,以……为准(有效)

All prices in the price lists are subject to our confirmation.

报价单中所有价格以我方确认为准。

The offer is subject to confirmation.

报价须经确认才有效。

④ confirmation [ˌkɒnfəˈmeɪʃən] *n.* 确认,回复

Once we received the confirmation, we will be able to proceed with your request.

一旦我们收到确认,我们将能够继续完成您的要求。

⑤ for your review   供您参考

I have attached my resume for your review.

在此我附上我的简历供您参考。

UNIT 2

【译文】

亲爱的克里斯：

  很高兴收到您关于我们156号这款印花衬衫的询价。

  我已经和我们经理商量过了，我们可以给您的最低价格是每打78美元，CIF温哥华，包括你们5%的佣金。最早的发货日期是5月12日。该报价以3月25日前你方确认为有效期。

  我们附上了156号印花衬衫的报价单，供您查看。样品可在4个工作日内准备好，请提供您的详细地址。

  我们期待着您的回复。

李安琪谨上

Part 3 实训

1. Translate the following sentences into Chinese.

（1）As we are in the market for wigs, we should be pleased to have your catalogue with price list for our consideration.

（2）Seeing your advertisement in a newspaper, we ask you to send us your latest price list, together with an illustrated catalogue.

（3）Please quote as requested in our inquiry sheet your lowest prices and state the earliest delivery date.

（4）If you are in a position to supply the goods as per (as per = according to) the attached enquiry at very competitive prices, we trust large orders will be obtained.

2. Translate the following sentences into English.

（1）我们对你方报价单里的西装有兴趣，请将报价单寄来。

（2）为了给你们提供更多有关我公司的信息，我们随函附上我们最新的小册子供你们参考。

（3）因事务紧急，我方盼望能在本周内收到贵公司的复函。

3. Translate this Chinese letter of inquiry into English.

敬启者：

  我们是这个城市防水服装（waterproof garment）的主要经销商。我们的顾客对贵公司生产的雨衣感兴趣，并曾询问过它们的品质。

  若质量和价格适宜，你们的雨衣在这里会有较好的销量。如你们能选一批男、女装雨衣寄来，并同意给我们14天的试销期（on fourteen day's approval），我们将非常感谢。在此期限结束时，任何未销出而我们又不准备作为库存的产品将退还给你们,退货费用由我方承担。
盼请早日赐复。

刘颂扬谨上

4. Write a letter of inquiry using the following information.

敬启者:
　　我们从网站得知贵公司是各种玩具的大出口商,我们在本地区是一家玩具的大经销商。
　　我们现在正在寻找一位供应商作为我们的长期合作伙伴。我们想请你方寄一份带价目表的商品目录,并报给我方你们到纽约的成本加保险费、运费的最低价。如果你方具有竞争力,我方将向你方大量订货。
　　由于事务紧急,我方盼望能在本周内收到贵公司的复函。

保罗·约翰逊谨上

【答案】

1. Translate the following sentences into Chinese.
(1) 我方正求购假发,请寄带价目表的商品目录以供我们参考。
(2) 看到你们在报纸上的广告,我们想请你方寄送产品的最新价目表,并附插图目录。
(3) 请按我们询价单中的要求报最低价,并说明发货日期。
(4) 如你方能按照我方随函附寄的询价单以具竞争性的价格供货,我们相信贵公司能获得我们的大量订单。

2. Translate the following sentences into English.
(1) We are interested in your suits in the sample book. We should be glad if you would send us your quotations.
(2) To give you more information about our company, we enclose our latest brochure for your reference.
(3) We look forward to receiving your reply within this week as the matter is urgent.

3. Translate this Chinese letter of inquiry into English.

Dear Sirs,
　　We are a leading dealer in waterproof garments in this city. Our customers have expressed interest in your raincoats and enquired about their quality.
　　Provided quality and price are satisfactory, there are prospects of good sales here.

> We should be thankful if you would send us, on fourteen day's approval, a selection of men's and women's raincoats. At the end of the period, any of the items unsold which we decide not to keep as stock, would be returned at our expense.
>
> We look forward to hearing from you soon.
>
> Yours sincerely,
> Songyang Liu

4. Write a letter of inquiry using the following information.

> Dear Sirs,
>
> We know from the website that your company is a big exporter of all kinds of toys. We are a big distributor of toys in our region.
>
> Now, we are looking for a supplier as our long-term partner. We would like to ask you to send us a catalogue with a price list and quote us your lowest cost plus insurance and freight rates to New York. If you are competitive, we will place a large order with you.
>
> As the matter is urgent, we look forward to receiving your reply within this week.
>
> Yours sincerely,
> Paul Johnson

Unit 3

报价与还价
（**Offer and Counter-offer**）

UNIT 3

Part 1　定义及写作步骤

1. 定义

报价(offer/quote)也称发盘或发价,一般由卖方给出,即卖方为发盘人,买方为受盘人。报价一旦由受盘人接受,便对双方构成约束力。

还价(counter-offer)是指受盘人不同意报价而提出变更意见。还价一旦提出,原报价将会失效。

注意:

(1) 报价(发盘)的内容必须十分确定,至少包括3个要素:商品的名称、数量、价格。

(2) 报价(发盘)必须标明"经受盘人接受,发盘人即受其约束"的意思。

(3) 报价(发盘)都具体规定一个有效期,作为对方表示接受的时间限制,超过发盘规定的时限,发盘人即不受其约束。

(4) 报价(发盘)有实盘(firm offer)和虚盘(non-firm offer)之分,两者的区别:虚盘意思表示一般很含糊,没有一个肯定的表示,如"中间价格""数量可能不会太多"等;商品的品质、数量、交货期、价格条款及付款方式等一般不齐全;有些发盘虽然意思明确,要素齐全,但带有一定的保留条件,也属于虚盘,如"以我方最后确认为准""以我方货物未先售出为准"及"仅供参考"等。

实盘:This offer is subject to your reply within 5 days.

This quotation is subject to your acceptance reaching us by 18th May.

This is our firm offer.

虚盘:Our offer is subject to goods being unsold.

This offer is subject to our final confirmation.

This quotation is subject to change without notice.

(5) 还价(还盘)过程中,如果受盘人对原发盘进行了实质性变更,就构成了对发盘的拒绝,其法律后果是否定了原发盘失效。实质性变更是指对商品的价格、付款方式、品质、数量、交货时间和地点、赔偿责任范围和争端解决办法等条件提出变更。

2. 写作步骤

1) 报价

(1) 感谢对方询价。

- Thank you for your inquiry of June 15.
- We warmly welcome your inquiry of April 4 and thank you for your interest in our products.
- We have received your letter dated on May 26, 2018 with many thanks.

(2) 报价内容(价格、折扣、付款方式、装运等细节)。

- In reply to your inquiry, we take pleasure in making you an offer as follows: In compliance with your request, we now offer you 1,000 dozen table-cloths, art No.142 for prompt shipment at USD15 per dozen CIF Long beach.

- We have pleasure in sending you here with the samples and a price list for…
- Our offer is USD300 per set of tape-recorder F.O.B. Tianjin.
- We enclosed our catalogs giving the details you asked for.

（3）报价期限。
- We are making you, subject to your acceptance before the end of this month, the undermentioned offer.
- Our offer is subject to your confirmation reaching here on or before the 25th March.
- We're willing to make you a firm offer at this price.

（4）期望。
- We feel confident that you will find the goods both excellent in quality and reasonable in price.
- We look forward to receiving your order.
- We hope you will find our quotation satisfactory and look forward to receiving your order.

2）还价

（1）感谢对方报价。
- Thank you so much for your offer.
- Thank you for your letter of June 16 offering us your raincoat.
- We appreciate your prompt response to our inquiry.

（2）解释还价原因。
- We like your raincoats, but your price appear to be on the high side as compared with those of other suppliers.
- In reply, we regrettably [rɪˈgretəblɪ]（抱歉地）state that our end-users here find your price too high and out of line with the prevailing [prɪˈveɪlɪŋ]（普遍的）market level.
- We know your goods are in high quality, but your price is 10% higher than your competitor.

（3）要求降价或提出其他条件。
- We do hope you kindly reduce the price by 5%.
- Should you be prepared to reduce your limit by, say 10%（将你的上限下调 10%，即降价 10%），we might come to term（合作）.
- May we suggest that you could perhaps make some allowance on your quoted prices?
- Taking into consideration the transport condition, we hope you can improve your packing so as to avoid damage to the goods.

（4）期望。
- We are anticipating your early reply.
- We hope our counter-offer will be acceptable to you and look forward to hearing from you.
- We regret to say that your price is on the high side, we do not think there is any possibility of business unless you cut your price by 20%.

必备词汇和句型

1. offer [ˈɒfə] v.& n. 报价,发价,发盘
   He will write Rachel a note and offer her a fair price for the land.
   他将给蕾切尔写一张便条,就那块土地开出合理的价格。
   make an offer   报价
   accept an offer   接受报价
   extend an offer   延长报价
   renew an offer   更新报价
   withdraw [wɪðˈdrɔː] an offer   撤销报价
   the validity [vəˈlɪdɪti] of an offer   报价有效期

2. counter-offer n. 还价,还盘
   We are sorry to tell you that we can not accept your counter-offer.
   非常抱歉地告诉你方,我方不能接受你方的还价。

3. competitive adj. (价格等)有竞争力的,竞争的,比赛的
   We are having to cut our costs to reduce overheads and remain competitive.
   我们现在必须减少开支以降低运营费用并保持竞争力。
   Are your products and services competitive?
   你们的产品和服务有竞争力吗?

4. allowance [əˈlaʊəns] n. 限额,折扣
   We can't make any allowance for this products.
   这批货我们不能再让价了。

5. stock n. 库存
   We took the decision to withdraw a quantity of stock from sale.
   我们决定将一批存货下架。

6. medium [ˈmiːdiəm] adj. 中等的,中级的
   The store sells big ones, small ones, medium ones, or whatever you want.
   那家商店卖大号的、小号的、中号的,应有尽有。

7. decline [dɪˈklaɪn] v.(在品格、价值上)降低 n. 下降
   The demand for our products suddenly begins to decline.
   我们产品的需求量突然下降。
   The market price of electronic components is on the decline.
   电子元件的市场价格一直在下降。

8. ready seller / quick seller / quick-selling product   畅销品
9. conclude business with sb.   与某人达成交易
10. close business/close a deal/close a transaction/close a bargain   达成交易
11. trade v.& n. 贸易,交易

trade terms   贸易条件   trade terms = trade conditions
trade agreement   贸易协定
trade fair   交易会
trade mark   商标
foreign trade   对外贸易
trade in sth.   经营某物
trade with sb.   与某人交易

12. **favourable** *adj.* 优惠的,有利的
    favourable price   优惠的价格
    favourable terms   优惠条件
13. **commission** [kəˈmɪʃən] *n.* 佣金(付给为卖方或买方服务的第三方费用)
    a commission of …% = …% commission   百分之几佣金
    your…% commission = your commission of …%   你的百分之几佣金
    The above price includes your commission of 2%.
    上述价格包括你方2%佣金。
14. general practice   惯例

Part 2 范例及讲解

1. 报价(Offer)
范例 1：Non-firm offer

From：Kelly Wang
To：Justin Bonder
Subject：Quotes for soybeans

Dear Justin,
　　We thank you very much for your inquiry of April 26 for soybeans.(感谢对方询价)
　　The **quality**① of soybeans is high, but the **quantity**② is not large enough to meet the demand because of the bad weather in the northeast of China. **Considering**③ our good relationship in business, we are giving you an offer as follows, **subject to**④ the products being unsold.(虚盘报价)
　　1000 **metric tons**⑤ of soybeans of first class at the lowest price of USD200 per metric tons CIF Boston, 5% **more or less**⑥ at seller's option.(报价)

> We look forward to receiving your early reply.(期望)
>
> Best regards,
> Kelly

【讲解】

① quality　*n.* 品质,质量　　high-quality goods 优质商品

Product quality suffers when costs are cut.

一降低成本,产品质量就会受到影响。

② quantity　*n.* 数量

We import huge quantities of oil each year.

我们每年进口大量石油。

③ consider　*v.* 考虑

considering　*prep.* 考虑到,就……而论

Considering the decline in the market, we suggest you cut your prices.

考虑到市场行情下滑,我方建议你方降价。

④ be subject to　受……的影响,以……为准

The prices of overseas holidays are subject to surcharges.

海外度假游的价格受各种附加费的影响。

The plan is subject to your confirmation.

这个计划以您的确认为准(需要您的确认)。

⑤ metric ton　公吨　实行公制的国家每公吨为 1000 千克

long ton　长吨　实行英制的国家每长吨为 1016 千克

short ton　短吨　实行美制的国家每短吨为 907 千克

⑥ more or less　或多或少,溢短装

溢短装条款是合同中规定卖方交货数量的浮动比例,在这个比例范围内多交(溢)或少交(短),均不算违约。

I've more or less finished reading the book.

我差不多已经把这本书全看完了。

10% more or less at the seller' option.

10%的溢短装由卖方选择。

【译文】

亲爱的贾斯廷：

非常感谢您4月26日关于大豆的询价。

大豆品质较高，但由于东北地区气候条件恶劣，数量不足以满足需求。考虑到我们在业务上的良好关系，我方向你方报盘如下，但以产品未售出为准。

购买1000公吨一等大豆的CIF波士顿价格为每公吨200美元，5%的溢短装由卖方选择。

期待着您的早日回复。

最好的问候

凯莉

范例2：Firm offer

From：Grace Wang
To：Alex Smith
Subject：Quotes for table-cloths art No. 125

Dear Alex,

　　We have received your letter of March 12 and are pleased to know your desire to enter into business relationship with us.（感谢对方询价）

　　In compliance① with your request, we now offer you USD20 per dozen CIF Long beach for 1000 dozen table-cloths, **art**② No. 125. This offer is subject to your **confirmation**③ before March 31.（实盘报价）

　　The price offered above is **reasonable**④. As the selling season is approaching, we have received many inquiries from other clients.（价格合理）

　　We enclose a commodity list and several pamphlets for your reference. Should you **find** any other **items**⑤ **of interest**⑥, please let us know and we will make your offers **promptly**⑦.（随附商品清单供参考）

　　We look forward to your early reply.（期望）

Best regards,
Grace

【讲解】

① compliance [kəmˈplaɪəns]　*n.* 服从，承诺，符合

UNIT 3

in compliance with… 遵从,服从

She gave up the idea in compliance with his desire.
她顺从他的愿望而放弃自己的主意。

All the cases are strongly packed in compliance with your request.
按你方要求,所有箱子都包装得很牢固。

② art n. 货品,物品(文中是指货品号 125 号)　　art = article

③ confirmation [ˌkɒnfəˈmeɪʃən] n. 确认,接受　　也可用 acceptance 或 reply

subject to your confirmation　经您确认才算有效(以您确认为准)

④ reasonable adj. 合理的,适当的

The refrigerator is reasonable in price.
这种电冰箱价格公道。

Aren't those all reasonable demands?
那些不都是合理的要求吗？

⑤ item n. 条款,项目,一件商品(或物品)

Leather jeans are the must-have fashion item of the season.
皮革牛仔裤是这一季必备的时尚服饰。

The other item on the agenda is the tour.
日程中的另一项是旅游。

⑥ find…of interest 对……感兴趣

⑦ promptly [ˈprɒmptlɪ] adv. 迅速地,毫不迟疑地

promptly = as soon as possible

If there is any difficulty, please let us know promptly.
倘若有困难,请迅速通知我们。

prompt adj. 敏捷的,迅速的,立刻的,准时的

Prompt payment of bills is greatly appreciated.
如蒙即期付款,则不胜感激。

【译文】

亲爱的亚历克斯:

我们已收到您 3 月 12 日的来信,很高兴知道您希望与我们建立业务关系。

为了满足您的要求,我们为您提供货号为 125 商品的报价:购买 1000 打桌布,CIF 长滩价格为每打 20 美元。此报盘以你方 3 月 31 日前确认为准。

以上价格合理。随着销售季节的临近,我们收到了许多客户的询价。

我们附上一份商品清单和几本小册子供您参考。如果您发现任何其他感兴

趣的商品,请告知我们,我们将尽快向您报价。

期待着您的早日回复。

格蕾丝谨上

2. 还价和回复(Counter-offer and reply)

范例1：Counter-offer

From：Alex Smith
To：Grace Wang
Subject：Re：Quotes for table-cloths art No. 125

Dear Grace,

　　I am sorry that we couldn't accept the price of USD20 per dozen which is rather too high for the market we wish to supply.

　　We have to **point out**① that these table-cloths are also **available**② in our market from some **native**③ manufactures, all of whom are at prices from 10% to 15% below the price you quoted.

　　Anyway, we would like to reduce our **margin**④ to establish our business. So we have to ask you to consider if you can make 10% **reduction**⑤ in your price.

　　Hope your early reply!

Yours sincerely,
Alex

【讲解】

① point out　指出,表明
It is hoped that the readers will kindly point out our errors.
希望读者指正。

② available　adj. 可得到的
This documents are available for download.
这些文件可以下载。

③ native　adj. 本地的,本国的
I'm a native of this place.
我是本地人。
Many of the plants are native to Brazil.
这些植物中有很多原产地在巴西。
The French feel passionately about their native tongue.

法国人对他们的母语非常热爱。

④ margin [ˈmɑːdʒɪn] *n.* 盈余,边缘,极限

profit margin　利润率

gross margin　毛利

a gross margin of 45%　45%的毛利

This false advertising hurts the profit margin of this company.

这种虚假的广告宣传影响了该公司的利润率。

She added her comments in the margin.

她在页边空白处加上了她的评语。

⑤ reduction　*n.* 降价,减少

reduction in　在……方面减少

Many companies have announced dramatic reductions in staff.

许多公司已经宣布大幅裁员。

They received a benefit in the form of a tax reduction.

他们获得了减税优惠。

【译文】

亲爱的格蕾丝：

　　对不起,我们不能接受每打 20 美元的价格,这对我们要供应的市场来说价格太高了。

　　不得不指出这些桌布在我们的市场上也可以从一些本地厂家买到,它们的价格都比你方报的低 10%～15%。

　　无论如何,我们想尽量减少自己的利润来建立我们的业务。因此,我们请您考虑是否可以将价格降低 10%。

　　希望您早日回复！

亚历克斯谨上

范例 2：Reply

From：Grace Wang

To：Alex Smith

Subject：Re：Quotes for table-cloths art No. 125

Dear Alex,

　　We have received your counter-offer of March 26 asking us to make 10% reduction in our price.

Much to our **regret**①, we are unable to **comply**② with your request because we have given you the lowest possible price. We have no margin to reduce the price again. We can assure you that the price we quoted **reflects**③ the high quality of the products.

I have discussed with our manager and decided that 2% will be provided as a special discount when quantity is up to 1500 dozens.

We hope to have the opportunity to cooperate with you.

Yours sincerely,
Grace

【讲解】

① regret [rɪ'gret]　*v.& n.* 遗憾,后悔
I regret to inform you this sorrowful news.
我很遗憾地通知你这个不幸的消息。
much to our regret = we feel sorry that　我们很遗憾(抱歉)

② comply [kəm'plaɪ]　*v.* 服从
comply with sth./sb.　服从某事/某人
You must comply with her request.
她的要求你应照办。

③ reflect [rɪ'flekt]　*v.* 反映,体现
Their actions clearly reflect their thoughts.
他们的行动清楚反映了他们的思想。

【译文】

亲爱的亚历克斯:

我们已收到您3月26日的还价,要求我们降价10%。

很遗憾,我们无法满足您的要求,因为我们已经给您尽可能低的价格。我们没有余地再降价了。我们可以向您保证,我们的报价反映了产品的高品质。

我和我们的经理商量过了,决定在数量达到1500打时给予您2%的特别折扣。

希望有机会与您合作。

格蕾丝谨上

Part 3　实训

1. Translate the following sentences into Chinese.

（1）In reply to your inquiry, we take pleasure in making you an offer as follows, provided your reply reaches us within 5 days from today.

（2）Unfortunately, your prices appear to be on the high side for garments of this quality.

（3）We suggest a reduction of 10% on orders of 1,000 metric tons.

（4）We offer you, subject to our final confirmation, the following goods.

2. Translate the following sentences into English.

（1）我同意您减价5元的还价。

（2）很抱歉,我们不得不拒绝你方发盘。

（3）除非你方减价5%,否则我们无法接受报盘。

3. Translate this Chinese letter of offer into English.

> 敬启者:
>
> 　　非常感谢收到您12月9日的询盘,并得知贵方对我方产品非常感兴趣。随附我公司的产品目录和价格清单,相信贵方一定会满意我们的产品和价格,本发盘限10日内复到有效。
>
> 　　再次感谢贵方对我方产品的兴趣,贵方一定会发现物有所值,期待贵方的订单。
>
> 李刚谨上

4. Write a letter of counter-offer using the following information.

> 敬启者:
>
> 　　感谢您提供的发盘,但经过我们仔细研究,我们发现你方价格太高,我们知道您的商品质量高,但与欧洲同类型产品价格相比,价格比您的竞争者高出5%~10%。因此,我们希望您能降价约5%,即每箱7.30美元。我们认为这项优惠你方应该会接受的。
>
> 特瑞西谨上

【答案】

1. Translate the following sentences into Chinese.

（1）兹答复贵方询盘,我方发盘如下,本发盘5日内复到有效。

(2) 可惜贵方这类服装的价格似乎偏高。

(3) 我方建议订货量超过 1000 公吨降价 10%。

(4) 我方对货物报价如下,以最后确认为准。

2. Translate the following sentences into English.

(1) I'll respond to your counter-offer by reducing our price 5 dollars.

(2) We regret that we have to decline your offer.

(3) We can't accept your offer unless the price is reduced by 5%.

3. Translate this Chinese letter of offer into English.

Dear Sirs,

　　We welcome you for your inquiry of December 9 and thank you for your interest in our commodities. We are enclosing some copies of our illustrated catalogues and a price list giving the details you asked for, and we trust that you will agree that our products and price appeal to the most selective buyer. This offer is subject to your acceptance within 10 days.

　　Thank you again for your interest in our products. We hope you will find our quotation satisfactory and look forward to receiving your order.

Yours sincerely,
Li Gang

4. Write a letter of counter-offer using the following information.

Dear Sirs,

　　Thank you so much for your offer, but after we carefully studied, we found your price is too high. We know that your goods are in high quality in comparison with the same items produced in Europe. However, your price is 5%~10% higher. So we do hope you kindly reduce the price approximately 5%, say USD7.30/ctn. I believe this concession should be acceptable by you.

Yours sincerely,
Tracy

Unit 4

付款方式
(Payment Method)

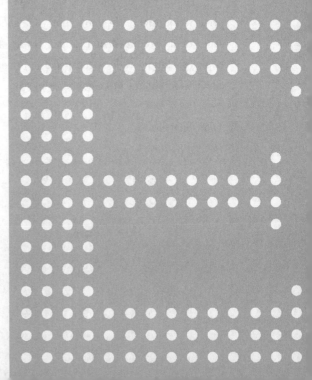

Part 1 定义及写作步骤

1. 定义

付款方式是外贸英语中作为谈判的重要因素,然而买卖双方常常在付款方式上无法达成一致。一封有效的国际商务函电能说服对方使用自己公司的付款方式,这既考验外贸人的英语水平,也在一定程度上决定订单的成功与否。

国际贸易的付款方式分为3种:汇付(remittance)、托收(collection)、信用证(L/C)。

(1) 汇付。汇付是指付款人通过银行,主动把款项汇给收款人的一种付款方式,最为快捷、省钱、方便。一笔汇款业务中涉及汇款人、汇出行、汇入行或解付行、收款人4个基本当事人,常用于买方的预付货款。通常应在合同中明确规定汇付的时间、具体的汇付方式和汇付金额等。例如:买方不迟于12月1日将100%的货款用电汇预付并抵达卖方。汇付的方式有如下3类,T/T最常用。

T/T——Telegraphic Transfer 电汇
D/D——Demand Draft 票汇
M/T——Mail Transfer 信汇

(2) 托收。托收是出口商为了向进口商收货款,开立汇票委托银行代收的结算方式。出口商将作为货物所有权的商业单据与汇票一起通过银行向进口商提示,进口商只有在承兑或付款后才能取得货权凭证。托收包括D/P和D/A。

D/P——Documents Against Payment 付款交单。付款交单是代收行必须在进口商付清货款后,才可将作为货物所有权的商业单据交给进口方的一种结算方式。根据汇票的期限,又可以分为即期付款交单和远期付款交单。

D/A——Documents Against Acceptance 承兑交单。承兑交单是出口商在装运货物后开具远期汇票,连同作为货物所有权的商业单据通过代收行向进口商提示,代收行在进口商对远期汇票加以承兑(即做出承诺)后即可将这些商业单据交给进口商,至汇票付款到期日,进口商才履行付款责任。

(3) 信用证。信用证是开证银行根据进出口商的要求和提示或代表其自身,开给出口商(受益人)的,在单证相符的条件下承诺支付汇票或发票金额的文件。常用的信用证有以下两种。

sight L/C 即期信用证
defered L/C 远期信用证

注意:

(1) 外贸实际操作中,最常见的付款方式T/T、L/C、D/P、T/T定金&尾款T/T、T/T定金&尾款信用证、T/T定金&尾款见提单副本。

(2) 信用证(L/C)是最常用的付款方式,可靠且安全,因为它引入银行作为第一付款人,尤其适用于陌生的买卖双方进行交易,对双方都有保障。买方开出信用证后,卖方按信用证所列要求发货后,向银行提交全套符合要求的单据后,银行就会无条件支付货款给卖方。

（3）付款交单（D/P）是通过银行托收，银行只负责托收单据的工作，对买方货款不予负责；而用信用证的情况下，开证行以自己的信用为交易垫付货款。就卖方的利益来说，尽量不选择D/P，选择D/P时务必确保托收银行是客户所在国家的知名银行。

（4）电汇（T/T）是最快速、方便、省钱的付款方式，但没有引入银行作为第三方参与者，因而适合于彼此熟知或互相信任的买卖双方。

2. 写作步骤

1) 买方提出付款要求

（1）提及货物、询盘、合同等。
- We refer you to your quotation.
  我们向您提及您的报价。
- With regard to our contract…
  关于我们……合同。

（2）提出付款方式及理由。
- As you know…so we prefer…
  你知道……因此我们倾向于……
- Owing to…we would appreciate it if you…
  由于……若……我们将非常感激。

（3）希望对方同意。
- We wish you can accommodate us in this respect.
  我们希望你方再次给予照顾。
- We hope to receive your favorable reply.
  我们希望早日收到你方答复。

2) 卖方回复付款信

买方提出一种付款要求，卖方可以同意也可以拒绝。

（1）表示收到信函。
- We have received your letter of…
  我们已经收到你方……的来信。
- Thank you for your letter…
  感谢你方……的来信。

（2）表明同意与否及理由。
- We agree to…
  我们同意……
- We regret being unable to accept…
  很遗憾我们不能接受……

（3）表明愿与对方合作的意愿和诚意。
- We extend you this accommodation in view of our relationship.
  鉴于我们的关系，我们愿给予您如此照顾（优惠）。
- We sincerely hope that we can…

诚挚地希望我们能……

必备词汇和句型

1. remittance [rɪˈmɪtəns] n. 汇付
   remit [riˈmɪt] v. 汇付
   telegraphic transfer (T/T) 电汇
   mail transfer (M/T) 信汇
   demand draft (D/D) 票汇
2. collection n. 托收
   remitting bank 托收行(卖方)
   collecting bank 代收行,汇付行(买方)
   documents against payment (D/P) 付款交单
   documents against acceptance (D/A) 承兑交单
3. L/C n. 信用证   L/C=letter of credit
   sight L/C=L/C at sight 即期信用证
   deferred [dɪˈfɜːd] L/C=L/C at ×× day's sight 远期信用证
   documentary credit 跟单信用证
4. modes of payment 付款方式
   terms of payment 付款条件
   外贸中,付款条件通常是指付款方式,即用什么方式(信用证,电汇,托收等)付款。
5. adopt v. 采用
6. performance bond 履约保证金
7. accompany [əˈkʌmpəni] v. 伴随
   be accompanied by 随附
8. sth. be on demand 需求……
9. draft=bill of exchange=bill 汇票(汇票是国际贸易中的重要单据)
   honor draft 承兑汇票
10. drawer n. (汇票)出票人
11. payer n. 付款人
    payee n. 收款人,被付款人
12. shipping documents 运输单据
13. down payment 预付款
14. commission [kəˈmɪʃən] n. 佣金
15. expire [ɪkˈspaɪə] v. 到期(失效)
16. on account of 由于……,因为……
17. comply [kəmˈplaɪ] v. 服从
    to be strictly complied with 已(被)严格履行

18. instruct [ɪnˈstrʌkt]　*v.* 指示
19. authorize [ˈɔːθəraɪz]　*v.* 授权
20. violate [ˈvaɪəleɪt]　*v.* 违背,违反　violation　*n.* 违反,践踏
21. abide (by) [əˈbaɪd]　*v.* 遵守
22. days of grace　宽限日期

Part 2　范例及讲解

1. 买方要求更易于接受的付款条款

From: Daniel Taylor
To: Dick Lin
Subject: Payment issue for artificial flowers

Dear Dick,

　　We refer you to your offer for **artificial flowers**① of the April 24. Having studied your quotation, we find the payment of a **confirmed**, **irrevocable L/C**② you **call for**③ is unacceptable.(说明对方的付款条款)

　　From the moment to **open credit**④ till the time our buyers pay us, the **tie-up**⑤ of our funds lasts about four months. At present, this question is particularly **taxing**⑥ owing to the **tight money condition**⑦ and the high bank interest. (解释这种付款方式不便的原因)

　　If you would kindly make easier payment terms, we are sure that such an **accommodation**⑧ would **be conducive to**⑨ encouraging business between us. We propose "**D/P at 45 day's sight**⑩". (具体付款要求)

　　Your kindness in **giving priority to the consideration of**⑪ the above request and giving us an early favorable reply will be highly appreciated. (希望早日获得回复)

Yours faithfully,
Daniel

【讲解】
① artificial [ˌɑːtɪˈfɪʃəl]　*adj.* 人造的,人工的,假的
artificial flowers　假花
He did not want his life to be prolonged by artificial means.
他不想靠人为方式延长生命。

They outfitted ['aʊtfɪd]（安装）him with artificial legs.

他们为他安了假腿。

② confirmed, irrevocable L/C 保兑的、不可撤销的信用证

A confirmed, irrevocable letter of credit is required.

要求用保兑的、不可撤销的信用证付款。

③ call for 要求

Your plan will call for a lot of money.

你的计划需要许多钱。

These wonderful results call for a celebration.

这些惊人的成绩值得庆祝一番。

④ open credit （买方）开立信用证　　credit＝letter of credit＝L/C　信用证

⑤ tie-up　n.（资金）积压,（交通）阻塞,（经济）合作

The heavy snowstorm caused a tie-up of traffic.

大风雪造成了交通的暂时阻塞。

The tie-up between the two natural resources firms was completed on 2 May.

这两家自然资源公司之间的合作已于5月2日完成。

⑥ taxing　adj. 繁重的, 费劲的

These taxing questions are too difficult for me to answer.

这几个思考题难度太大了, 我不会解答。

It's unlikely that you'll be asked to do anything too taxing.

不大可能让你去做什么太费劲的事情。

⑦ tight　adj. 紧的, 紧张的

tight money condition　货币紧缩

⑧ accommodation [ə͵kɒmə'deɪʃn]　n. 住处, 调节, 和解

His instinct would be to seek a new accommodation with the colleagues.

他本能的反应会是寻求与同事们取得新的和解。

Unprincipled accommodation will do harm to him.

无原则的迁就对他有害。

⑨ be conductive to　有助于

To lead a regular life is conducive to good health.

规律起居有恒有益健康。

This is conducive to the sustainable development of global and regional economies.

这有利于世界和地区经济的可持续发展。

⑩ D/P at 45 day's sight　买方见到卖方单据及汇票后45天之内付款交单

此外, 还有 D/P at sight（即期付款交单）, 即见到卖方的单据及汇票后买方立刻付款。

⑪ priority [praɪ'ɒrəti]　n. 优先

giving priority to the consideration of　优先考虑

Our first priority is to improve standards.

我们的头等大事是提高水平。

【译文】

亲爱的迪克：
　　请查阅您4月24日关于假花的报价。经研究，我们不能接受您要求的保兑的、不可撤销的信用证这种付款方式。
　　从开立信用证到买家付钱给我们，我们的资金积压大约持续4个月。在当前形势下，由于货币紧缩和高昂的银行利率，这个问题越发严重。
　　如果贵方能简化付款条件，我们确信贵方这样的安排将有助于促进我们之间的贸易。我们提议"见票后45天内付款交单"。
　　如能优先考虑上述要求，及早给予有利的答复，我们将不胜感激。

丹尼尔谨上

2. 卖方拒绝对方付款方式

From：Dick Lin
To：Daniel Taylor
Subject：Re：Payment issue for artificial flowers

Dear Daniel,
　　We thank you for your order of artificial flowers and appreciate your **intention**① to **push**② the sales of our products in your country.
　　However, your suggestion of payment by D/P at 45 day's sight is unacceptable. Our usual **practice**③ is to accept orders against confirmed, irrevocable L/C at sight, and valid for 3 weeks after shipment is made. We also allow **transshipment and partial shipments**④.
　　As per⑤ the above terms we have done **substantial**⑥ business. We hope you will not **hesitate**⑦ to come to the agreement with us on payment terms so as to get the first transaction **concluded**⑧.
　　Your favorable reply will be highly appreciated.

Yours faithfully,
Dick

【讲解】
① intention　*n.* 意向，意愿

intention to do sth. 有意向做某事

② push *v.* 推销,促进

push the sales of the products 推销产品,促进销量

③ practice *n.* 做法,实践

He has a chance to put his new ideas into practice.

他有个机会实施他的新想法。

④ transshipment and partial shipments 转运和分批装运

The carrying vessel shall be provided by the seller. Transshipment is allowed and partial shipments are not allowed.

载运船只由卖方安排。允许转船,但不允许分批装运。

⑤ as per 根据,按照   as per = per

⑥ substantial [səbˈstænʃəl] *adj.* 大量的

substantial business 大量的业务

That is a very substantial improvement in the present situation.

在当前形势下这是一个非常巨大的进步。

He made substantial donations to charity.

他为慈善事业捐了很多钱。

⑦ hesitate [ˈhezɪteɪt] *v.* 犹豫

don't hesitate to do sth. 毫不犹豫地做某事

In the event of difficulties, please do not hesitate to contact our Customer Service Department.

如果遇到困难,请与我们的客户服务部联系。

She hesitated a long time and then she said "Yes".

她犹豫了很长时间,然后才说"行"。

⑧ conclude [kənˈkluːd] *v.* 完成,达成

get the first transaction concluded 完成第一次交易

(get sth. done 短语结构,使……被完成,完成……)

【译文】

亲爱的丹尼尔:

感谢您订购假花并有意向在贵国推销我们的产品。

但是,你方建议见票后45天内付款交单,这是不能接受的。我们通常的做法是接受保兑的、不可撤销的即期信用证,在装船后3周内有效,允许转运和分批装运。

根据上述条款,我们已经做了大量工作。希望您能就付款条件与我们达成协议,以便达成第一笔交易。

UNIT 4

如蒙回复,将不胜感激。

迪克谨上

3. 卖方同意对方付款方式

From: Dick Lin
To: Daniel Taylor
Subject: Re: Payment issue for artificial flowers

Dear Daniel,

Thank you for your order of artificial flowers. Your **proposal**① of paying by D/P at 45 day's sight has been carefully **studied**② by us.

Usually, this method is not acceptable to us. However, in view of our long pleasant relations as well as our willingness to support our African friends, we agree with you this time.

But let us make it clear that this accommodation is only for this transaction, which will **in no case**③ set a **precedent**④.

Attached is our Sales Contract No.105 covering the above order. Please follow the usual **procedure**⑤.

Yours faithfully,
Dick

【讲解】

① proposal [prə'pəuzəl] *n.* 建议,提案,求婚
This proposal has been voted down.
这一提案已被否决。
After a three-weekend courtship, she accepted Jason's proposal of marriage.
经过3个周末的追求之后,她接受了杰森的求婚。

② study *v.& n.* 研究,学习
They totally overlooked the study of the subject.
他们完全忽视了对此问题的研究。

③ in no case 无论如何,在任何情况下都不能
I will reveal your secret in no case.
无论如何我都不会说出你的秘密。
In no case can you cheat in the exams.

无论如何你都不能考试作弊。

④ precedent ['presɪdənt] *n.* 先例

set a precedent 开创先例,提供先例

This decision set a precedent for future cases of a similar nature.

这一裁决为今后性质类似的案件提供了先例。

There are plenty of precedents in that company for letting people out of contracts.

在那家公司,允许员工解除合同的先例有很多。

⑤ procedure [prəˈsiːdʒə] *n.* 程序,过程

It has passed through an interesting procedure of evolution.

它经过了一个有趣的进化过程。

【译文】

> 亲爱的丹尼尔:
> 　　感谢您订购假花。我们已经仔细研究了你方45天内付款交单的建议。
> 　　通常我们无法接受延期信用。但鉴于我们长期愉快的关系以及我们支持非洲朋友的意愿,我们这次同意您的要求。
> 　　但是,请允许我们明确表示,这种调整仅适用于这一次交易,下不为例。
> 　　随函附上我方关于上述订单的第105号销售合同。请按常规程序办理。
>
> 　　　　　　　　　　　　　　　　　　　　　　　　　　　　迪克谨上

Part 3　实训

1. Translate the following sentences into Chinese.

(1) We will not pay until shipping documents for the goods have reached us.

(2) We've drawn on you for payment of the invoice amounting to USD30,000.

(3) We should be obliged for your immediate amendment of the L/C to enable us to make shipment in time.

(4) We do not agree to change the terms of payment from L/C at sight to D/P at sight.

2. Translate the following sentences into English.

(1) 开即期信用证是我方对所有客户的要求。

(2) 我们不能接受延期付款。

(3) 这是国际贸易中惯用的付款方式。

(4) 由于开证延误,不能按合同进行装运,要推期至10月。

UNIT 4

3. Translate this Chinese letter into English.

亲爱的巴雷特：
　　感谢您订购200台23A46号空调,并感谢您推动我方产品在贵国的销售。但是,你方关于电汇付款的建议是不可接受的。我们的惯例是凭保兑的、不可撤销的即期信用证接受订单,有效期为装运后3周,并允许转船和分批装运。我们已经按上述条款做了大量的生意。希望贵方能毫不犹豫地就付款条件与我方达成协议,以便达成第一笔交易。
　　如蒙回复,将不胜感激。

林希谨上

4. Write a letter of reply using the following information.

你是王双,请写一封给买方Joe的回复信,拒绝买方4月30日来信中要求的D/A付款方式,告知对方需要用L/C付款方式。

【答案】

1. Translate the following sentences into Chinese.

(1) 见不到货物装船单据,我们不会付款。
(2) 我们已经按照发票金额30 000美元向你方开出了汇票。
(3) 如你方能立即修改信用证使我方能及时装运,我们将不胜感激。
(4) 我们不同意将即期信用证付款方式改为即期付款交单。

2. Translate the following sentences into English.

(1) L/C at sight is what we request for all our customers.
(2) We can't accept payment on deferred terms.
(3) This is the normal terms of payment in international business.
(4) Owing to the delay in opening L/C, shipment cannot be made as contracted and should be postponed to October.

3. Translate this Chinese letter into English.

Dear Barrett,
　　We thank you for your order NO.23A46 for 200 air conditioners and appreciate your intention to push the sales of our products in your country. However, your suggestion of payment by T/T is unacceptable. Our usual practice is to accept orders against confirmed irrevocable L/C at sight, valid for 3 weeks after shipment is made and allow transshipment and partial shipments. As per the above terms we have done substantial business. We hope you will not hesitate to come to agreement with us on

payment terms so as to get the first transaction concluded.

Your favorable reply will be highly appreciated.

Yours sincerely,
Xi Lin

4. Write a letter of reply using the following information.

Dear Joe,

We have received your letter dated April 30. We regret that we are unable to consider your request for payment on D/A terms. You are well aware that our usual terms of payment are by L/C, which have been widely accepted by large customers in your country. For your information, great demand has result in price rise. Your early decision is necessary. We look forward to your early.

Yours sincerely,
Shuang Wang

Unit 5

订单与确认
(Orders and Acknowledgment)

Part 1 定义及写作步骤

1. 定义

订单是指买方对指定货物确认购买的一种表示。它可以是对卖方发盘的接受,也可以根据卖方提供的商品目录、价格表和样品直接订购。

确认是指卖方收到买方订单后表示接受或者拒绝的行为。

注意:

(1) 订单的内容必须十分清楚和确定,订单中必须包含如下内容。

① 详细的货物信息,包括货物的数量、等级、尺寸、颜色、型号等。

② 表明货物的包装方式、装卸港口和装运期。

③ 货物的价格和付款方式等。

(2) 若因市场行情的变动等原因想要拒绝买方订单,一定要语言谨慎、语气委婉,着眼于以后的长远合作。

(3) 订单一旦被确认接受,对双方都有约束力,双方都要保证合同的顺利履行。

2. 写作步骤

1) 买方下订单

(1) 承接之前邮件,对产品满意决定订购。

- Thank you for your letter of June 12, and we find both quality and prices satisfactory and are pleased to give you an order.
- We thank you for your letter of September 4 and we are glad to inform you that your samples are satisfactory.
- Our customers are very interested in your samples of bed-sheets, and enclosed is our order.

(2) 订单具体内容。

① Name of commodity.

② Quantity: a. case of wine; carton of cigarettes; bale of paper; drum of beer etc.

　　　　　　b. metric ton; long ton; short ton etc.

　　　　　　c. dozen; gross; piece; pair etc.

③ Quality: a. grade A, B, C etc.

　　　　　　b. large, medium, small etc.

　　　　　　c. 2.5m×3m etc.

④ Price: USD500 per metric ton CIF London.

⑤ Packing.

⑥ Time of shipment.

(3) 结束语。

- All these items are urgently required by our customers, therefore, we hope you will make the delivery at an early date.

- We hope this first order may lead to the further business between us.
- Please send us your confirmation of sales in duplicate.

2）卖方确认订单

（1）感谢买方的订单。

- Thank you very much for your order No.3428 for 3000 pieces of bed-sheets.
- We have received your letter of May 24 informing us you are satisfied with our products. Thank you for your repeat order.
- We are very pleased to receive your order of October 18 and welcome you as one of our customers.

（2）对订单表示接受或者拒绝。

- Your order is receiving our immediate attention, and you can depend on us to effect the delivery well within your time limit.
- We regret that we can't confirm the order at the prices we quoted 6 weeks ago, since the cost of materials has risen substantially [səb'stænʃəli].
- Your order is confirmed and will be handled with great care. Please open relevant L/C, which must reach us one month before the time of shipment.

（3）期望。

- We shall be pleased to receive your further orders.
- Would this be acceptable? Please let us know if you wish to change the order.

必备词汇和句型

1. order *n.* 订单 *v.* 订购

   place an order   订购

   on order   订购中，已订购

   This item is out of stock, but it is on order.

   这项产品全部售空（已无存货），但已经订购了。

   accept an order   接受订单

   cancel an order   撤销订单

   confirm an order   确认订单

   execute an order   履行订单

   a back order   尚未执行的订单

   a fresh order   新订单

   a repeat order   续订订单

   British Rail are going to place an order for 188 trains.

   英国铁路公司将订购188列火车。

   They can't supply our order.

   我们订的货他们无法供应。

The airlines still have 2500 new aeroplanes on order.
这家航空公司尚有 2500 架新飞机在订购中。

2. stipulation [ˌstɪpjʊˈleɪʃən] *n.* 约定,条款
   The shipper always asks the opening bank to delete this stipulation.
   托运人总是要求开户行删除这一条款。
   The general L/C usually bears this stipulation.
   公开信用证通常带有这个条款。

3. conform [kənˈfɔːm] *vi.* 符合,遵照
   conform to 符合;与……一致
   in conformity with… 和……相适应,和……一致
   The package does not conform to EU rules.
   这种包装不符合欧盟规定。
   The plan was made in conformity with his views.
   仍按他的意见制订计划。

4. confirm [kənˈfɜːm] *v.* 确认
   confirmation [ˌkɒnfəˈmeɪʃən] *n.* 确认,认可
   We're waiting for written confirmation from the Americans.
   我们在等美国人的书面确认。
   We need confirmation in writing before we can send your order out.
   给你们发送订购的货物之前,我们需要书面确认。

5. acknowledgment [əkˈnɒlɪdʒmənt] *n.* 承认,确认书
   I have received neither an acknowledgment nor a reply.
   我未收到任何回复或答复。

6. satisfactory [ˌsætɪsˈfæktəri] *adj.* 令人满意的,符合要求的
   This bicycle is quite satisfactory—just the thing I want.
   这辆自行车买得很称心。

7. effect [ɪˈfekt] *v.* 使发生,实行 *n.* 效果,影响,印象
   Prospects for effecting real change seemed to have taken a major step backwards.
   实现真正改变的机会似乎变得更加渺茫了。
   The illness had a profound effect on his outlook.
   这场病对他的人生观产生了深刻的影响。

8. term *n.* 条款,术语,方面,(合同、保险的)有效期
   in terms of 在某个方面
   Our goods compete in terms of product quality, reliability and above all variety.
   我们的产品在质量、可靠性,尤其是品种方面颇具竞争力。
   Premiums are guaranteed throughout the term of the policy.
   在保单有效期内,所缴纳的保险费是有保障的。

9. **considerable** [kənˈsɪdərəbə] *adj.* 相当大(多)的,应考虑的
Quite a considerable number of interviews are going on.
大量的采访在继续。

与品质(quality)有关的词

1. specifications 规格
2. grade 等级
3. standard 标准
4. sample 样品
5. colour sample 色彩样品
6. pattern sample 款式样品
7. original sample 原样
8. duplicate sample 复样
9. counter sample 对等样品
10. reference sample 参考样品

11. sealed sample 封样
12. representative sample 代表性样品
13. catalogue 商品目录
14. pamphlet 宣传小册子
15. description 说明书
16. tolerance 公差
17. article No. 货号……
18. assortment 花色(搭配)
19. 5% plus or minus 增减5%
20. fair average quality 平均质量

与数量(quantity)有关的词

1. weight 重量
2. metric ton 公吨
3. long ton 长吨
4. short ton 短吨
5. kilogram/kilo/kg 千克
6. pound/lb 磅(1磅≈0.45千克)
7. ounce/oz 盎司(1盎司≈0.028千克)
8. number 个数
9. piece 件
10. pair 双
11. dozen 打
12. ream 令
13. set 套
14. length 长度
15. area 面积

16. volume 体积
17. cubic meter 立方米
18. capacity 容积
19. litre 升
20. gallon 加仑
21. bushel 蒲式耳
22. metric system 公制
23. British system 英制
24. American system 美制
25. gross weight 毛重
26. net weight 净重
27. shipping weight 装运重量
28. landed weight 卸货重量
29. theoretical weight 理论重量

与包装(packing)有关的词

1. packaging 包装方法
2. blister packing 起泡包装
3. neutral packing 中性包装
4. skin packing 吸塑包装
5. hanging packing 挂式包装
6. catch sb's eye 引某人注目

7. mark　唛头
8. unlabelled packing　无牌的包装
9. in bulk　散装
10. in loose packing　散装
11. nude packing　裸装
12. bulk pack　整批包装
13. consumer pack　零售包装
14. large packing　大包装
15. inner packing/external packing/end packing　小包装
16. shrunk packaging　压缩包装
17. foam-spary packaging　喷泡沫包装
18. gift-wrap　礼品包装
19. bag/sack　袋
20. jute bag　麻袋，polybag　胶袋
21. polythelene bag/plastic bag　塑料袋
22. polythelene net　尼龙绳网袋
23. zippered bag　拉链袋
24. case/chest　箱
25. box　盒
26. wooden case　木箱
27. carton　纸箱
28. container　集装箱
29. crate　板条箱
30. fibre board case　纤维板箱
31. packet　小包
32. bale　包
33. bundle　捆
34. tin/can　罐头
35. basket　篮,篓,筐
36. bamboo basket　竹篓
37. bottle　瓶
38. wooden keg　小木桶
39. hogshead　大桶
40. iron drum　铁桶
41. cylinder　气缸
42. barrel　琵琶桶
43. drum　圆桶
44. waterproof paper　防水纸
45. cellophane　玻璃纸
46. kraft paper　牛皮纸
47. canvas　帆布
48. fibreboard　纤维板
49. nylon strap　尼龙带
50. plastic strap　塑料带
51. adhesive tape　胶带
52. stuffing material　填料
53. nylon plastic　尼龙丝
54. fermented plastic　泡沫塑料
55. paper scrap　纸屑
56. saw dust　木屑
57. slushing compound　润滑油

Part 2　范例及讲解

1. 订单（Orders）

To：Lily He
From：Ben Smith
Subject：Order No. 358 for 100% cotton towel

Dear Lily,
　　Thank you for your offer on August 8 for the 100% cotton towel. We find both

UNIT 5

quality and prices satisfactory and are pleased to give you an order for the following items:

Purchase order

Anxin Trading co.ltd

Order No. 358

Date: August 10, 2018

Model No.	Description①	Size	Color	Quantity/pieces	Unit price②(FOB)	Total
Y001	100% cotton towel for adults	34cm×73cm	colors	2,000	USD2	USD4,000
Y002	100% cotton towel for kids	25cm×50cm	colors	2,000	USD0.5	USD1,000

Packing: Each piece in a **polybag**③, 100 pieces in a **carton**④.

Payment: L/C.

Shipment: From Qingdao to Rotterdam.

All these items are urgently required by our customers, so we hope you confirm our order and make delivery as soon as possible.

Best regards,

Ben

【讲解】

① description [dɪˈskrɪpʃən] *n.* 描述,形容,说明

description of goods 货物名称,货物摘要

According to the description of the goods, the goods can be packed in crates.

根据对商品的描述,上述产品可以用条板箱包装。

② unit price 单价

Our standard unit price to the wholesaler is USD23.5.

我们给批发商的标准单价是 23.5 美元。

③ polybag [ˈpɒlɪbæg] *n.* 塑料袋,胶袋

Each shirt is packed in a polybag and 6 to a box.

每件衬衫装一个塑料袋,6 袋装一盒。

④ carton [ˈkɑːtn] *n.* 纸箱

When the postal clerk delivers your order, check the carton before signing for it.

你订购的货物由邮政人员送达时,要先检查一下包装盒再签收。

Unit 5　订单与确认

【译文】

亲爱的莉莉：

　　谢谢您 8 月 8 日 100%纯棉毛巾的报价。我们对质量和价格都感到满意,很高兴向你们订购下列商品：

采购订单

安信贸易有限公司　　　　　　　　　　　　　　　　　　358 号订单

　　　　　　　　　　　　　　　　　　　　　　　　日期：2018 年 8 月 10 日

型号	说明	尺寸	颜色	数量/件	单位价格（FOB）/美元	合计/美元
Y001	100%成人棉毛巾	34cm×73cm	多色	2000	2	4000
Y002	100%儿童棉毛巾	25cm×50cm	多色	2000	0.5	1000

包装：一个塑料袋装 1 件,1 箱 100 件。
付款方式：信用证。
运输：从青岛到鹿特丹。
所有这些产品都是我们客户急需的,所以我们希望你们确认订单,并尽快交货。

　　　　　　　　　　　　　　　　　　　　　　　　　　　最好的问候

　　　　　　　　　　　　　　　　　　　　　　　　　　　本

2. 确认（Acknowledgment）

To：Ben Smith
From：Lily He
Subject：Re：Order No. 358 for 100% cotton towel

Dear Ben,

　　We are very pleased to acknowledge your order No.358 of August 10 for 100% cotton towel and enclosing herewith our **S/C**① No.759 in duplicate. Please sign and return one copy to us for our **files**②.

　　As to the terms of payment, we would like you to open an **irrevocable**③ L/C strictly confirm to the terms stated in our Sales Conformation. We will **take the responsibility**④ to **effect**⑤ the shipment **upon**⑥ receipt of your L/C.

　　If there is anything in problem, do not hesitate to let us know.

Best regards,
Lily

【讲解】

① S/C　*n.* 销售确认书,销售合同

S/C＝sales confirmation（销售确认书）＝ sales contract（销售合同）

S/C 是买卖双方在通过交易磋商达成交易后,由卖方出具并寄给双方加以确认的列明达成交易条件的书面证明,经买卖双方签署的确认书,是法律上有效的文件,对买卖双方具有同等的约束力。

② file　*v.* 把……归档　*n.* 文件(夹),档案

I looked your address up in the personnel file.

我在人事档案里找到了你的地址。

③ irrevocable　*adj.* 不能取消的,不可撤销的

The bank has made out an irrevocable letter of credit.

银行开出了不可撤销的信用证。

不可撤销信用证是指开证行一经开出、在有效期内未经受益人或议付行等有关当事人同意,不得随意修改或撤销的信用证;只要受益人按该证规定提供有关单据,开证行(或其指定的银行)保证付清货款。

④ take the responsibility　负责

We can also take the responsibility of chartering a ship.

我们也可以负责租船装运。

⑤ effect　*v.* 使发生,实行　*n.* 效果,影响,印象

Prospects for effecting real change seemed to have taken a major step backwards.

实现真正变革的前景似乎倒退了一大步。

⑥ upon　*prep.* 基于……,在……之上

Upon seeing her, I smiled and ran toward her.

一看到她我就笑着跑了过去。

【译文】

亲爱的本:

　　我们非常高兴收到你方 8 月 10 日的第 358 号 100% 棉毛巾的订单,并随函附上我方第 759 号销售确认书,一式两份。请签名并退回一份给我们存档。

　　关于付款方式,我们希望您尽快通过贵方银行开立不可撤销的信用证。信用证中的所有规定都应严格按照销售合同中规定的条件付款。收到你方信用证后,我方将负责装运。

　　如果有什么问题,尽管告诉我们。

最好的问候

莉莉

Unit 5 订单与确认

Part 3 实训

1. Translate the following sentences into Chinese.

（1）I have pleasure in ordering the following products.

（2）We find your terms satisfactory, please make the delivery as soon as possible.

（3）We received your order but would like to make a small change.

（4）We wish to point out that the L/C clauses should totally conform to our sales contract.

2. Translate the following sentences into English.

（1）因原材料短缺,工厂将不得不拒绝贵方的订单。

（2）贵方能在收到订单后5周内完成交货吗？

（3）如果首次订单进展顺利,我们会考虑后期进一步的合作。

3. Translate this Chinese letter into English.

敬启者：
　　我方已经收到贵方128号关于床单的订单,但是因为原材料价格上涨我们不得不对价格做一下小的调整,我方在3月28日给出的报价是每套25美元,你方能否接受每套30美元的新报价？如果可以的话,我方将对订单进行确认。
　　对此造成的不便我方深表歉意,期待贵方的尽快答复。

　　　　　　　　　　　　　　　　　　　　　　　　　　　　　　刘盼谨上

4. Translate this English letter into Chinese.

Dear Ms. Smith,

　　Your offer for the T-shirts on May 20 gained our best attention, we would like to order the following items：

　　Large 2000 dozen

　　Medium 4000 dozen

　　Small 2000 dozen

　　As the sales season is approaching, the total order quantity should be shipped in July. At that time an irrevocable L/C for the total purchase value will be opened. Please confirm this order as soon as possible.

Best regards,
Xinzhuo Zhao

UNIT 5

【答案】

1. Translate the following sentences into Chinese.

(1) 兹订购下列产品。

(2) 我们对条款内容非常满意,请尽快交货。

(3) 我方已收到贵方订单,但仍需做一些小的调整。

(4) 请贵方注意信用证的条款内容必须与我们的销售合同完全一致。

2. Translate the following sentences into English.

(1) Because of the shortage of raw materials, our manufactures have to decline the orders.

(2) Could it be possible for you to deliver within 5 weeks when you receive the orders?

(3) If the first order is satisfactorily executed, we shall place further orders with you.

3. Translate this Chinese letter into English.

> Dear Sirs,
>
> We have received your order No.128 for bed-sheets, but we would have to make a small change in price because of the raw materials has risen since we offered you USD25 per unit on March 28. We wonder if you can accept the new offer USD30 per unit, then we will acknowledge your order.
>
> We are really regretful for this inconvenience and look forward to your early reply.
>
> Yours faithfully,
> Pan Liu

4. Translate this English letter into Chinese.

> 亲爱的史密斯女士:
>
> 贵方5月20日的关于体恤的报价引起了我方极大兴趣,我方决定订购如下货物:
>
> 　　大号 2000 打
> 　　中号 4000 打
> 　　小号 2000 打
>
> 因销售旺季即将到来,请务必将货物于7月完成装运。同时,我方也会开好按购买金额的不可撤销的信用证。请尽快对订单进行确认。
>
> 　　　　　　　　　　　　　　　　　　　　最好的问候
> 　　　　　　　　　　　　　　　　　　　　赵心卓

Unit 6

保险
（Insurance）

Part 1　定义及写作步骤

1. 定义

　　保险是指投保人/被保险人(the insured)在货物装运前向承保人/保险人/保险公司(insurer)投保,办理保险手续(insurance formalities)、选择保险险别(coverage)、确定保险金额(insurance amount)、支付保险费(insurance premium)并领取保险单证(insurance documents)的过程。

　　保险合同(insurance contract)常采用保险单(又称为大保单,insurance policy)的形式,是承担风险的承保人和寻求防御风险的投保人之间的合同。若投保的风险发生了,承保人为报偿投保人所付的保险费,同意付给投保人一笔规定的金额。

注意：

　　(1) ICC(Institute Cargo Clauses)为伦敦保险协会保险条款。CIC(China Insurance Clauses)为中国保险条款。PICC(The People's Insurance Company of China Limited)为中国人民财产保险股份有限公司。参照ICC制定的各种涉外保险业务条款,总称为CIC。

　　(2) 我国的保险分为基本险(basic risks)和附加险(additional risks)。基本险有3种：①平安险(Free from Particular Average, FPA)；②水渍险(With Particular Average, WPA)；③一切险(all risks)。

　　附加险包括一般附加险(general additional risks)和特殊附加险(special additional risks)。一般附加险包括偷窃、提货不着险(Theft, Pilferage and Non-Delivery, TPND)、淡水/雨水损坏险(fresh water or rain damage risk)、短缺险(shortage risk)、铁锈险(rust risk)等。特殊附加险包括战争险(war risk)、罢工险(strike risk)、进口税险(import duty risk)、交货不到险(failure to deliver risk)、火险(fire risk)等。

　　(3) 对于FOB和CFR合同,由进口方对货物投保并支付保险费。对于CIF合同,一般由出口方按发票金额的110%投保一切险,110%由100%的CIF金额和10%的合理利润及其他费用组成。有时进口方要求投保金额超过110%,额外保险费应由进口方承担。

　　(4) 保险费是指投保人向保险公司缴纳的钱。保险金额是指发生事故后,保险公司依据合同给投保人的钱。如出口方购买某保险花2000元,这个金额就是保险费；投保人的货物发生意外,保险公司理赔20 000元,这个金额则是保险金额。

　　(5) 我国出口贸易中最常使用CIF术语,即我国出口方按照进口方要求办理保险。所以进口方常常会通过邮件形式表达他们对保险的具体要求。

2. 写作步骤

1) 买方写保险信

(1) 提及货物、询盘、合同等。

- We refer you to your quotation.
  我们参考你方报价。
- With regard to our contract⋯
  关于我们……的合同。

（2）提出保险要求及理由。

- As…we shall be glad if you…
  因为……如果你……我们将不胜感激。
- As you know…we suggest…
  你知道……我们建议……
- Owing to…we would appreciate it if you…
  由于……如果你……我们将不胜感激。

（3）希望对方同意。

- We wish you can accommodate us in this respect.
  我们希望你方在此方面给予照顾。
- We hope to receive your favorable reply.
  我们希望早日收到你方答复。

2）卖方回复保险信

（1）表示收到信函。

- We have received your letter of …
  收到你方……的来信。
- Thank you for your letter …
  感谢你方……来信。

（2）表明同意与否及理由。

- We agree to…
  我们同意……
- We regret being unable to accept…
  很遗憾我们不能接受……
- We want to make it clear that…
  我方想澄清一点……

（3）表明愿与对方合作的意愿和诚意，如表示会立即发货等。

- We sincerely hope that we can…
  诚挚地希望我们能……
- We have insured the goods…
  我们已经为货物投保……

必备词汇和句型

1. insure [ɪnˈʃʊə] v. 保险，投保，保证
   insure sth. 为……买保险
   insure against sth. 买保险以避免……
   We can insure your belongings against fire and theft.
   我们能够为您的财产投保火灾险和失窃险。

Think carefully before you insure against accident, sickness and redundancy.
在为意外事故、疾病与失业投保之前一定要考虑清楚。

2. insurance [ɪnˈʃʊərəns] premium [ˈpriːmiəm] 保险费
3. insured amount / insurance amount / insurance value 保险金额
4. the insured / insurance applicant 投保人/被保险人
5. insurer / underwriter 承保人(保险人)
   large underwriters 大保险公司(大保险商)
6. cover / effect / arrange / take out insurance 投保
7. handled insurance against 投保
   handled insurance against all risks = cover all risks 投保一切险
8. insurance coverage / risks covered 保险范围
9. insurance policy = policy 保险单
10. insurance clause 保险条款
11. insurance instruction 投保通知
12. customary [ˈkʌstəməri] adj. 习惯的,通常的
    He carries himself with his customary elegance.
    他保持着一贯的温文尔雅。
    At Christmas it was customary for the children to perform bits of poetry.
    圣诞节孩子们总要唱一些圣诞颂歌。
13. invoice [ˈɪnvɔɪs] value 发票金额
14. process [ˈprəʊses] n. 过程
15. encounter [ɪnˈkaʊntə] v.& n. 遇到
    Every day of our lives we encounter stresses of one kind or another.
    我们生活中的每一天都会面临这样或那样的压力。
    The author tells of a remarkable encounter with a group of Chinese dancers.
    作者讲述了和一群中国舞者的奇遇。
16. in such circumstances [ˈsɜːkəmstɑːns] 在这种情况下
17. for one's account 由……承担
18. percentage [pəˈsentɪdʒ] 百分比
19. Ocean Marine Cargo Clauses 海洋运输货物保险条款
20. ICC(Institute Cargo Clauses) 伦敦保险协会保险条款
21. CIC(China Insurance Clauses) 中国保险条款
22. PICC(The People's Insurance Company of China Limited) 中国人民财产保险股份有限公司
23. coverage [ˈkʌvərɪdʒ] n. 保险项目(险别),范围,规模,(新闻)报道
    This is an insurance policy with extensive coverage.
    这是一项承保范围广泛的保险。

There're coverage of foreign news on this channel.
这个台有国外的新闻报道。
24. in the absence of   在没有……情况下
25. accordingly   （用在句尾）照办，（用在句首）因此
26. breakage   *n.* 破损，破碎险
27. undergo [ˌʌndəˈɡəʊ]   *v.* 经受
When people feel under threat, they undergo physical and mental changes.
当人们感到受到威胁时，他们会经历身体和心理上的变化。
28. rough [rʌf] handling   野蛮装卸

Part 2　范例及讲解

1. 来信提出保险要求

To: Lily He
From: Ben Smith
Subject: Insurance issue

Dear Lily,

　　Regarding S/C No. 759 for 4000 pieces of 100% cotton towels, we have established with **Barclays Bank PLC.**① in a confirmed, irrevocable L/C No.7726 **amounting to**② **STG**③ 6000 with **validity**④ until October 31. （通知对方信用证已开出）

　　Please **see to** it **that**⑤ the above-mentioned goods are shipped before October 13 and **insured**⑥ against **all risks**⑦ for 120% of the **invoice**⑧ value. We know that according to your usual practice, you insure the goods only for 10% over the invoice value, therefore the extra **premium**⑨ will be **for our account**⑩. （具体投保要求）

　　Please arrange the insurance as requested and in the meantime, we await your **shipping advice**⑪. （希望对方尽早安排投保和装运）

Best regards,
Ben

【讲解】
① Barclays Bank PLC.　巴克莱银行，位于英国
PLC 是 Public Company Limited 的缩写，翻译为公共有限公司。
② amount to   总计，金额达……

UNIT 6

Their loss amounts to USD8,000.

他们的损失达 8000 美元。

③ STG　*n.*英镑　STG＝Sterling

④ validity　*n.*有效期　valid　*adj.*有效的

The validity date of the L/C should be extended to April 30.

信用证有效期应延长到 4 月 30 日。

⑤ see to it that　确保

Please see to it that the goods are shipped as soon as the letter of credit reaches you.

请确保一收到信用证就装运货物。

⑥ insure　*v.*投保,办保险　　insurance　*n.*保险,保险费

Please insure for 10% above invoice value.

请按发票金额的 110%投保。

Insure for 10% above/over invoice value(＝Insure for 110% of the invoice value).

We shall provide such insurance at your cost.

我们会提供这样的保险,费用由您承担。

⑦ all risks　一切险,综合险　　risk　*n.*风险

They will not take any risk.

他们不愿冒任何风险。

⑧ invoice　*n.*发票　　commercial invoice　商业发票

⑨ premium　*n.*保险费　　insurance premium＝insurance＝premium

The extra premium is for buyer's account.

额外的保险费由买方承担。

⑩ for our account　由我方承担　for one's account＝on one's account　由……承担

We can insure the goods for your account.

若您承担费用,我们可为你投保。

⑪ shipping advice　装运通知

装运通知指卖方发货后向买方发出的通知,其内容包括货物名称、数量、金额、载货船名和开航日期等。

【译文】

亲爱的莉莉：

关于我们向您订购 4000 条 100%棉毛巾的第 759 号合同,我们已与巴克莱银行开立了保兑的、不可撤销的第 7726 号信用证,金额为 6000 英镑,有效期至 10 月 31 日。

请注意,上述货物应在 10 月 13 日前装运,并按发票金额的 120%投保一切险。我们明白按您的惯例,您只按发票金额的 110%投保,因此额外的保险费将由我们承担。

请按要求办理保险,同时,我们等待您的装船通知。

最好的问候

本

2. 卖方回复买方的保险信

To：Ben Smith
From：Lily He
Subject：Re：Insurance issue

Dear Ben,

　　This is to **acknowledge the receipt of**① your E-mail of August 27 requesting us to **effect**② insurance on the 4,000 pieces of 100% cotton towels.(表示收到对方保险要求的来信)

　　We are pleased to inform you that we have **covered**③ the above **shipment**④ with The People's Insurance Company of China against all risks for 120% of the invoice value instead of 110%. As you have mentioned, the extra premium will be for your account. The **policy**⑤ is being prepared and will be **forwarded**⑥ to you by the end of the week.(表明已按对方要求投保)

　　We are making **arrangements**⑦ to ship the 4,000 **pieces**⑧ of cotton towels from Qingdao Port. The ship will **sail**⑨ on or about the October 13.(通知对方将安排装运)

Yours sincerely,
Lily

【讲解】

① acknowledge　*v.* 确认,承认
acknowledge the receipt of=be in receipt of　前者较正式,表示收到
We acknowledge the receipt of your letter of April 3 2019.
我们收到您2019年4月3日的来信。
② effect=make　*v.* 使生效,办理
effect shipment/payment/insurance
Payment should be effected within 3 months after shipment.
需在发货后3月内付款。
③ cover=insure　*v.* 投保,办保险
We shall cover all risks for you.

我们将为你方投保一切险。
We shall cover the insurance ourselves.
我们将自己投保。

④ shipment　n. 装运,此处指一批货物
We received the shipment today.
我们今天收到了货物。

⑤ policy　n. 保险单　　policy = insurance policy

⑥ forward ['fɔːwəd]　v. 转交,转告
We will forward your decision to the buyers.
我们会把你们的决定转告买方。

⑦ arrangement　n. 安排
make arrangement to do sth.　安排做某事
We will make all necessary arrangements to deliver the goods in time.
我们将及时做出必要的安排,以便及时交货。

⑧ piece　n. 件,类似有 set(套)、case(箱子)、carton(纸箱)、tin(罐)

⑨ sail　v. 启航,开航
The ship is scheduled to sail for Singapore on June 23.
该轮船将于6月23日驶往新加坡。

【译文】

亲爱的本:
　　已收到您8月27日的邮件,要求我们对4000条100%棉毛巾投保。
　　我们很高兴地通知您,我们已向中国人民财产保险股份有限公司按发票金额的120%投保了上述货物的一切险,而不是110%。如您所说,额外保险费将由贵方承担。保单正在准备中,并将于本周末前转发给您。
　　我们正在安排从青岛港装运4000条棉毛巾。该船将于10月13日左右开航。

莉莉谨上

Part 3　实训

1. Translate the following sentences into Chinese.

(1) We have learned that the rate for all risks insurance on the computers consigned to New York is 1.5%. Please let us know whether we can cover insurance elsewhere at a more reasonable rate.

(2) This rate is generally adopted by all the large underwriters here.

（3）We want the insurance to be covered for 130% of the invoice value.

（4）The insurance premium for war risk is increasing enormously due to the prospect of war.

（5）We would like you to insure against strikes risk on the shipment.

2. Translate the following sentences into English.

（1）关于第345号合约项下的300台缝纫机,我们将自行办理保险。

（2）根据你们通常的CIF条件,所保的是哪些险别?

（3）我们将为货物投保CIF的110%,如果要求额外险别,则额外保费由买方承担。

（4）我们已经向中国人民财产保险股份有限公司办理了投保一切险,保险金额为25 000元。

（5）我们要求你方为我方货物投保水渍险,金额为20 000元。

3. Translate this Chinese letter into English.

敬启者:

现提及在CIF条件下有关500箱瓷器的第77号订单。如果您能按发票金额的150%投保一切险加破碎险为我方投保,我方将不胜感激。请确保货物在5月16日前装运。我们知道,按照你方惯例,你方只按多于发票金额的10%(即发票金额的110%)投保。因此,额外的保费将由我们承担。我希望这能得到贵公司的同意。

杰西卡谨上

4. Write a letter of insurance using the following information.

请以进口商Kevin的身份要求出口商对78号订单下的2000副眼镜按照发票金额的130%投保水渍险和破碎险。由于合同的价格是CIF,出口商通常的做法是按照发票金额的110%投保平安险或水渍险,请去信解释,并表达愿意配合但是额外的费用须由对方承担。

【答案】

1. Translate the following sentences into Chinese.

（1）据了解,运往纽约的计算机的一切险费率为1.5%。请告知我们能否以更合理的费率在其他地方投保。

（2）这个费率通常是所有大保险公司都采用的。

（3）我方希望按发票金额的130%投保。

（4）由于战争的可能性很大,战争险的保险费正在大幅增加。

（5）我们希望你方为货物投保罢工险。

2. Translate the following sentences into English.

（1）As to 300 sets of sewing machines under contract No.345, we would cover insurance on our own account.

（2）What is the coverage according to your usual CIF terms?

（3）Insurance on the goods shall be covered by us for 110% of the CIF value, and any extra premium for additional coverage, if required, shall be for buyer's account.

（4）We have handled insurance against all risks with PICC for RMB25,000.

（5）We request you to cover WPA on our cargoes for the amount of RMB20,000.

3. Translate this Chinese letter into English.

> Dear Sirs,
>
> I would refer you to your order No.77 for 500 cases of chinaware which is placed on CIF term. I would appreciate it if you insure against all risks plus risk of breakage for 150% of invoice value. Please ensure that the goods are shipped before May 16. As we know, according to your usual practice, you only insure for 10% above the invoice value (that is, 110% of the invoice value). Therefore, the extra premium will be borne by us. I hope this will meet your approval.
>
> Yours faithfully,
> Jessica

4. Write a letter of insurance using the following information.

> Dear Sirs,
>
> We wish to refer you to Order No.78 on 2,000 pairs of eyeglasses which is placed on CIF term. We would like to tell you that our usual practice is to insure FPA or WPA at 110% of the invoice value. Since you desire to effect insurance against WPA and breakage for 130% of the invoice value, we shall be pleased to comply, but you have to bear the difference in premium. We trust the above information will serve your purpose and we await your prompt reply.
>
> Yours faithfully,
> Kevin

【译文】

> 敬启者：
>
> 请确认订购2000副眼镜的第78号合同，您可以看到这个交易是在CIF基础上订立的。我们想告诉您，通常我们的做法是按发票金额的110%投保平安险或

水渍险。既然你想按照发票金额的130%为眼镜投保水渍险和破碎险,我们乐意遵守,但贵方要承担保费的差价。我们相信上述信息将对贵公司有用,我们期待您的及时回复。

凯文谨上

Unit 7

装运
(Shipment)

Part 1　定义及写作步骤

1. 定义

装运是国际贸易合同中卖方最基本的义务之一,是指卖方要在规定的时间、以合适的方式完成货物的运输工作。国际贸易的主要运输方式是海运,主要涉及装运期的规定、装卸港的选择、船运公司的选择、运费确定、运输单证的流转以及运输中出现问题的解决。

注意:

(1) 关于装运期的规定,装运期是指卖方在装运港装运货物的时间,具体的规定方法有3种。

① 规定具体的装运时间,如规定一段时间或者规定最迟的期限。

Time of shipment: May 16.

Time of shipment: not later than May 31/on or before May 31.

② 规定收到信用证后几天装运。

shipment within 30 days after receipt of L/C.

③ 规定近期装运,术语不建议采用:prompt shipment/shipment as soon as possible.

(2) 分批装运(partial shipment)和转运(trans shipment)。

分批装运是指一个合同项下的货物分若干批装运。但是,在不同时间将不同港口的货物装在同一航次、同一条船上,由于这条船上的货物同时到达目的港,不能称为分批装运。根据《UCP600》的规定:允许分批装运。

转运是指一个合同下的货物从装运地到目的地的运输过程中,中途需要转换运输工具。根据《UCP600》的规定:允许转运。

(3) 装船通知也称装运通知,是卖方的基本义务,除了便于交接货物外,主要表明其交付货物的风险已转由买方负责,在FOB和CFR贸易中,装船通知的作用更为重要,卖方及时发出装船通知以便买方及时办理货物运输保险。

(4) 装运港(port of loading)和卸货港(port of discharge)。

在买卖合同中,可以规定一个具体的装卸港口,也可以规定两个或两个以上的装卸港口,选择装卸港口的时候一定要注意有无重名的问题。

(5) 提单(B/L)和海运单(SWB)。

提单是证明海上货物运输合同和货物由承运人接管或装船,以及承运人据以保证交付货物的凭证。提单作为物权凭证是可以转让的,它是海运中非常重要的业务单证和法律文件。根据实际业务需要,有时船运公司也可签发海运单,海运单是记名的,不是物权凭证不能转让,提单和海运单只能选择其中一个。

2. 写作步骤

(1) 承接之前邮件,引出此次邮件主题。

- Thank you for your letter of July 6, asking us to quote you for container shipment to London for ten cartons of art goods.
- Your letter of June 12 has had our best attention. We apologize for the delay of the

shipment.
- We learn from your shipping advice that the goods we ordered on April 9 has been shipped by M/V Rotterdam.
- As requested in your letter of August 16, we wish to inform you that we have just received your amendment(修改) to the captioned(标题中的) L/C.

(2) 提出问题或者解决问题的方法。
- When you received the L/C, please effect the goods as soon as possible.
- As soon as the shipment is effected, would you please advise us of the name of the vessel(船), the voyage number(航次), the container number(集装箱号) immediately?
- We take this opportunity to inform you that we have shipped the above goods on M/V Taishan, which will sail for your port tomorrow morning.

(3) 期望。
- It is our sincere hope that this order will lead us to further business.
- We enclosed a copy of our freight quotation(运费报价) and look forward to receiving your further instructions.
- We assure you of our prompt and careful attention in handling your future orders.

必备词汇和句型

1. deliver [dɪˈlɪvə] *v.* 交货,发货
   delivery *n.* 交货,发货
   port of delivery   交货港
   time of delivery   交货期
   prompt [prɒmpt] delivery   即期交货
   make delivery   办理交货
   postpone [pəʊsˈpəʊn] delivery   推迟交货

2. shipment *n.* 装运,装载的货物
   The goods are ready for shipment.
   货物备妥待运。
   Please advise the date of shipment as soon as possible.
   请尽快通知装运日期。
   make shipment   装船
   receive shipment   接货
   prompt shipment   即期装运
   time of shipment   装运期
   partial [ˈpɑːʃəl] shipment   分批装船

3. freight [freɪt] *n.* 货物,货运 *v.* 运送
   On the customs declaration, the sender labeled the freight as agricultural machinery.
   在报关单上,发货人将货物列为农用机械。

The ocean freight of this 20' container is about USD1,200.
这个20英尺(1英尺=30.48厘米)集装箱的海运费约为1200美元。

4. consignment [kən'saɪnmənt] *n.* 装运/托运的货物,托运

The first consignment of food has already left Bologna.
运送的第一批食品已经离开了博洛尼亚。
We must ask you to dispatch the consignment immediately.
我们必须要求你方立即发送该批货物。

5. amendment [ə'mendmənt] *n.* 修改

He tried to push the amendment through Parliament.
他力促议会通过该修正案。

6. captioned ['kæpʃənd] *adj.* 标题中的

We are sending you herewith a duplicate copy of the captioned payment order.
我们随同寄上标题中的付款通知副本。

7. effect [ɪ'fekt] *v.* 使发生,引发,实现 *n.* 效应,影响

effect the change 实现改变
effect the shipment 发货

8. vessel ['vesəl] *n.* 容器;船

9. voyage ['vɔɪ-ɪdʒ] *n.* 航行,旅行

voyage number 航次

10. container [kən'teɪnə] *n.* 容器,集装箱

container number 集装箱号

11. sail [seɪl] *v.* 航行,起航

sail number 封条号
We decided, more or less on a whim, to sail to Morocco.
我们航海去摩洛哥的决定多少有点心血来潮。

12. delay [dɪ'leɪ] *v.& n.* 推迟,拖延

We'll send you a quotation without delay.
我们会立刻送一份报价给您。
Unfortunately, the delivery has been delayed due to the bad weather.
不幸的是因为天气原因,交货期延迟。

13. ensure [ɪn'ʃʊə] *v.* 确保,保证

We will try our best endeavors to ensure it doesn't happen again.
我们要全力保证此事不再发生。
Ensure that it is written into your contract.
确保把这一点写入合同中。

14. dispatch [dɪ'spætʃ] *v.& n.* 派遣,调度,(迅速地)发出

We have 125 cases ready for dispatch.
我们有125箱货准备发出。

15. delete v. 删除
    The shipper always asks the opening bank to delete this stipulation.
    托运人总是要求开户行删除这一条款。
16. regard v.& n. 涉及,至于,关于
    as regards to 至于,关于
    As regard to the job, I feel satisfied with it.
    至于我的工作,我觉得挺满意的。

Part 2 范例及讲解

1. 催促装运(Urging an early shipment)

To：Evan Jiang
From：George Bell
Subject：**Urging**① an early shipment

Dear Evan,
　　Referring to our order No. 189 for 2,000 pieces Bed-sheets, in which we decided the time of shipment was May, now we should have to remind you that time of shipment has been **pressing**②.
　　When we placed the orders we pointed out that **punctual**③ shipment is very important because the **dealer**④ is our largest and we assured that we could supply the goods before the end of June.
　　Your delay may cause us much inconvenience, so we want to know if you can arrange the shipment as soon as possible and we would ask you to be particularly careful to **seal**⑤ each piece into **water-tight**⑥ bag before packing into the cartons.
　　Please let us know immediately once the goods have been dispatched. All the relevant documents should be mailed by special express when they are ready.
　　Thank you for your cooperation.

Yours faithfully,
George

【讲解】
① urge [ɜːdʒ] v.&n. 催促,推进,要求
I urged him to finish his studies.
我催促他完成学业。

He had an urge to open a shop of his own.
他很想自己开一家店。

② pressing *adj.* 紧迫的, 紧急的

It is one of the most pressing problems facing this country.
这是该国面临的最紧迫的问题之一。

There is a pressing need for more funds.
迫切需要更多的资金。

③ punctual *adj.* 严守时刻的, 准时的

She is punctual in paying her bills.
她按期付款。

④ dealer *n.* 商人, 经销商

Can you recommend a reputable second-hand car dealer?
你能推荐个名声较好的二手汽车商吗?

⑤ seal [siːl] *v.* & *n.* 密封

He sealed the envelope and put on a stamp.
他封住信封并贴上一张邮票。

She merely filled the containers, sealed them with a cork, and pasted labels on it.
她只是装满容器, 用软木塞封住, 然后贴上标签。

When assembling the pie, wet the edges where the two crusts join to form a seal.
在包馅饼时, 先把两片馅饼皮边沿接头部分弄湿, 再将其捏合。

⑥ water-tight *adj.* 不透水的, 防水的   water-tight = waterproof

Be sure this kind of bags is water-tight.
请确保包装袋子是密封不透水的。

It is completely waterproof, light and comfortable.
它防水性能非常好, 而且轻巧、舒适。

【译文】

亲爱的埃文:

　　参照我方第189号订购2000件床单的订单, 我们将装运时间定在5月, 现在我们需要提醒您装运时间非常紧迫。

　　我们当时下订单时强调, 准时装运很重要, 因为经销商是我们最大的客户, 我们已承诺能在6月底前供货。

　　您的延误会给我们带来很多不便, 所以我们想知道您是否能尽快安排装运, 并且请在装箱前仔细将每件货物封入防水袋中。

　　货物发出请立即通知我们。所有相关文件准备好, 请立即用特快专递寄出。

　　谢谢您的合作。

乔治谨上

2. 修改运输条件（Amending shipping terms）

To: Leslie Wood
From: Mike Leng
Subject: Amending shipping terms

Dear Leslie,

　　Referring to the cargo of order No.576, **due to**① a **strike**② at Los Angeles port, which shows no sign of **letting up**③ for some time, we have to ask you to amend your L/C for the destination to Tacoma instead of Los Angeles through your bank.
　　We will try our best to guarantee the time of shipment.
　　Please let us know if we can change the port of destination as soon as possible.

Yours faithfully,
Mike

【讲解】

① due to…　由于,应归于　　due to…＝because of…
Due to the heavy rain, she can not go out to play.
因为大雨,她不能出去玩了。

② strike [straɪk]　n. 罢工(课、市)
The rail strike is causing major disruptions at the country's ports.
铁路罢工使该国港口陷入了一片混乱。

③ let up　放松,减少
The rain had let up.
雨势已经减弱。

【译文】

亲爱的莱斯利：
　　关于第576号订单的货物,由于洛杉矶港发生了罢工,这段时间一直没有停止的迹象,我们不得不要求您通过贵方银行将信用证上的目的地由洛杉矶改为塔科马。
　　我们将尽力保证装运时间。
　　如果能尽快更改目的港,请告诉我们。

迈克谨上

Unit 7 装运

3. 装运通知（Shipping advice）

To: Jason Hall
From: Harry Wei
Subject: Shipping advice

Dear Jason,
 We are very pleased to inform you that the following articles under our Contract No. 472 have been shipped on **M/V**① Florida, which will sail from Qingdao to Los Angeles on June 11.
 Enclosed please find all relevant documents:
 (1) Commercial Invoice in **duplicate**②.
 (2) One copy of packing list.
 (3) Ocean B/L in **triplicate**③.
 (4) One copy of Insurance Policy.
 It is pleasure to go business with you, and we hope that the goods will reach you in good time and meet your satisfaction.

Best regards,
Harry

【讲解】

① M/V 商船，货轮

M/V 的全称为 Merchant Vessel（商船）或 Motor Vessel（轮船），加在船名之前，译为"……轮"或"……船"。

M/V Anthas carried a shipment of sugar from Santiago de Cuba to Xingang.

"安塔斯"号轮载有一批食糖从古巴圣地亚哥驶往新港。

② duplicate *adj.* 完全一样的，复制的，副本的 *n.* 完全一样，副本

This form should be filled out in duplicate.

要填写这种表格，一式两份。

③ triplicate *adj.* 三倍的，一式三份的 *n.* 一式三份

Please fill in the remittance slip in triplicate.

请您填写汇款凭证，一式三份。

【译文】

亲爱的杰森：
 我们很高兴地通知您，根据我方第 472 号合同，下列货物已装运到"佛罗里达"

UNIT 7

轮,该船将于6月11日从青岛开往洛杉矶。
　　随函附上所有相关文件,请查收：
　　(1) 商业发票一式两份；
　　(2) 装箱单一份；
　　(3) 海运提单,一式三份；
　　(4) 保险单副本一份。
　　很高兴和你们合作,我们希望货物能及时到达,并满足你们的要求。

最好的问候
哈利

4. 电放(Telex release)

To：Eric Jones
From：Harry Wei
Subject：**Telex release**① to XYZ Co.ltd

Dear Eric,
　　We UVW Co.ltd confirm and hereby **authorize**② a telex release of the above mentioned cargo for which we **surrender**③ all sets of original B/L (**duly endorsed**④) and you are to **release**⑤ the containers to XYZ Co.ltd.
　　We accept full responsibility and all consequences for this release of the cargo in this manner, with no liability to OPQ shipping company, their principals or agent. The remaining original bills of lading are to be considered now **null and void**⑥ and are now of no value.

Best regards,
Harry

【讲解】
这是卖方 UVW 有限公司写给承运人(船运公司)OPQ 公司,请求其将货物电放给买方 XYZ 公司。
　　① telex release　电传放行(简称电放)
电放是指托运人(发货人)把货物装船后,将承运人(船运公司)所签发的全套正本提单交回船运公司,同时指定收货人(非记名提单的情况下)；承运人(船运公司)将电放提单的复印件发给收货人,并通知目的港的船运公司机构,只要收货人出具电放提单的复印件就可将货物交给他。

提单是物权凭证,买方只有拿到提单正本才能在目的港提货。电放意味着卖方放弃正本提单(original B/L),买方只要有电放提单的复印件或传真件就可以提货。有时,运输时间较短的货物可能采用电放提单,如中国到日本的货。但是卖方必须有把握收回货款,从而避免买方提货后不付款。如果需要做电放,卖方要向承运人出具一份电放保函,表明同意电放某笔提单,一切后果自己承担。

② authorize ['ɔːθəraɪz] *v.* 授权,批准,委托
He said that he needed to get his supervisor to authorize my refund.
他说必须让主管人员批准我的退款。

③ surrender [sə'rendə] *v.* 提交,交出
They have been ordered to surrender their passports.
他们被要求出示护照。

④ endorse [ɪn'dɔːs] *v.* 背书(背书就是转让的意思),签名
duly ['djuːli] *adv.* 及时,适当地
duly endorsed 适当背书
endorsement *n.* 背书
The payee of the cheque must endorse the cheque.
收款人必须在支票上背书。

⑤ release [rɪ'liːs] *v.* 放货,放开
He stopped and faced her, releasing her wrist.
他停下来面对着她,放开了她的手腕。

⑥ null [nʌl] and void [vɔɪd] *adj.* 无效的,失效的
The agreement will be considered null and void.
该协议将被视作无效。

【译文】

亲爱的艾瑞克:

我们 UVW 有限公司确认并在此授权上述集装箱/货物的电传放行,我们交出所有原始提单(正式背书),请把货物放行给 XYZ 有限公司。

我们对此次发布的货物承担全部责任和所有后果,OPQ 运输公司及其负责人或代理商不承担任何责任。剩余的原始提单现在应视为无效,且已无任何价值。

最好的问候

哈利

UNIT 7

Part 3 实训

1. Translate the following sentences into Chinese.

(1) We hope you will have the goods ready for shipment when you receive the letter.

(2) Please make your best efforts to get the goods dispatched with the least possible delay.

(3) We take pleasure to inform you that the goods under S/C No.378 have been dispatched on May 16 by M/V Marina.

(4) Please inform us the name of the carrying vessel, the departure and arrival time.

2. Translate the following sentences into English.

(1) 因无直接到达船舶,我方将安排货物从深圳转运。

(2) 载货船舶是欧洲轮,我们会尽快把提单传给您。

(3) 对于发运这批货物造成的延迟,我们感到十分抱歉。

3. Translate this Chinese letter into English.

> 亲爱的海伦:
>
> 　　我们已收到您3月25日的来电,要求我们尽快安排第786号订单的装运事宜。
>
> 　　很遗憾,我们联系了船运公司,由于近期港口拥堵,船舶仍在锚地等候靠泊。还需2~3天才能开始装货。一旦货物发运我们会尽快通知你。
>
> 　　再次对交付延误表示抱歉。
>
> 　　　　　　　　　　　　　　　　　　　　　　　　　　　　　　　　　　　刘明谨上

4. Write a letter of shipment using the following information.

> 亲爱的露西:
>
> 　　现告知您第5423号订单的黑茶质量受到我方客户的青睐,对方是我们在欧洲市场最大的客户。请尽快将货物通过马士基的船舶发运到安特卫普。
>
> 　　货物完成装运后,请尽快告知船舶名称、航次号、箱号和封条号,以及货物预计的到港时间。请谨慎处理货物的包装并保证产品质量。
>
> 　　希望我们有长期的合作。
>
> 　　　　　　　　　　　　　　　　　　　　　　　　　　　　　　　　　　　马敏谨上

【答案】

1. Translate the following sentences into Chinese.

(1) 我方希望你方收到这封邮件的时候,已经安排好货物的装运。

（2）请尽快完成货物的装运工作。

（3）兹通知第378号合同的货物已于5月16日装载于"马丽娜"号船舶发运。

（4）请告知载货船舶名字、离港和到港时间。

2. Translate the following sentences into English.

（1）Since there is no direct ship sailing for your port, we have to have the goods transshipped via Shenzhen.

（2）The carrier of the goods is M/V Europe, and we will send you the relevant B/L to you as soon as we receive it.

（3）We are very sorry for the delay of this consignment.

3. Translate this Chinese letter into English.

Dear Helen,

　　We have received your letter of March 25 requesting us earlier delivery of the goods under your purchase order No.786.

　　We have contacted with the shipping company and regret to tell you that the ship is still waiting at the anchorage for berth because of the port congestion. There is still another two or three days to commence loading. We will inform you immediately once the goods have been dispatched.

　　We are really very sorry for the delay.

Yours sincerely,
Ming Liu

4. Write a letter of shipment using the following information.

Dear Lucy,

　　We are pleased to inform you that the quality of the China dark tea under order No.5423 has met the requirement of our end-user, who is one of the largest tea buyers in Europe. Would you please ship the order to Antwerp via Maersk as soon as possible?

　　When the shipment is effected, would you please advise us the name of vessel, the voyage number, container number and seal number, as well as the estimated time of arrival? We would be grateful if you could give special care to the quality and the packing of the order.

　　It is our sincere hope that this order will lead to further business between us.

Yours truly,
Min Ma

Unit 8
索赔与处理
(Claims and Settlement)

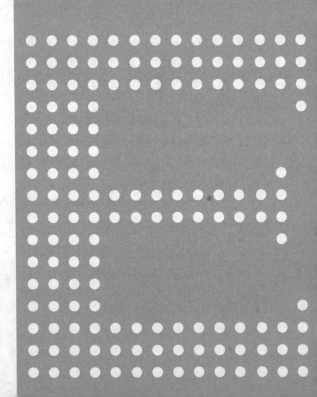

Part 1 定义及写作步骤

1. 定义

索赔（claims）是指受损方向违约方索要赔偿，而理赔（claims settlement）则是指违约方处理受损方的索赔要求。索赔和理赔是一个问题的两方面，在受损方是索赔，在违约方是理赔。外贸业务中，受损方通常是买方。买方索赔的原因：

(1) 买方不满意货物的质量或卖方的服务。
(2) 卖方发错或迟交货物。
(3) 货物受损或卖方价格过高等。

其中，最常遭投诉的一般是货物的质量问题。

买方索赔的要求：

(1) 要求赔偿（品质不符等）。
(2) 要求补运（短少或短交等）。
(3) 要求调换或维修（货物的品质不符或发生损坏等）。
(4) 要求减价或折让（交货延迟、品质不符等）。
(5) 拒收并退货，同时要求赔偿（品质严重不符等）。

另外，当买方信用证有误、未按时付款等，卖方也可能向买方提出索赔。当承运人（船运公司）有责任时，买方或卖方也会向承运人（船运公司）提出索赔。

注意：

(1) 买方写索赔邮件时，语气应礼貌缓和，措辞谨慎，客观公正地解释发生的情况，清楚地说明造成的损失以及要求的赔偿，做到有理有据、具体详细，这样才更容易获得对方的理解和赔偿。
(2) 索赔应该立即提出，拖延会给双方带来更大的麻烦。
(3) 卖方必须耐心谨慎地处理投诉和索赔，才不会影响和买方的合作关系。

在处理索赔时，应该记住下列重要的原则：①若卖方不能立即处理索赔，也要立即回信表示对对方的索赔正在处理中。②如果是卖方责任，应承认并深表歉意，并承诺纠正自己的错误；若不是卖方责任，则应说明拒绝理赔的理由。③不管卖方同意理赔还是拒绝，都应感谢买方告诉你事实。

2. 写作步骤

1) 买方的索赔信

(1) 详细说明问题。

- We regret to inform you that…
  我们很遗憾通知你方……

- We have just received…evidencing…
  我们刚收到……证明……

- Half of the packages had been broken.
  一半货物的包装破损。

UNIT 8

- It was found that upon examination…
  检查后发现……

（2）该问题带来的损失。

- The goods are rejected by our customers.
  我们的客户不接受这批货。
- This has caused us much inconvenience.
  这给我们带来了很大不便。

（3）希望对方如何解决。

- We look forward to your settlement at an early date.
  我们盼早日收到你方的解决办法。
- We wish to get your early reply.
  我们希望早日收到你方的答复。

2）卖方的理赔信（接受或拒绝）

（1）接受。

① 表示歉意。

- We are sorry for the late delivery of…
  我们为迟交……感到非常遗憾。
- We regret the inconvenience you have experienced.
  我们对给你方带来的不便表示遗憾。

② 解释原因并同意索赔。

- We went into this matter immediately and found that…
  我们立刻展开调查并发现……
- The wrong goods could be returned.
  发错的货可以退回。
- We are prepared to make you a reasonable compensation.
  我们准备给你方合理的赔偿。

③ 希望继续合作。

- We wish to be able to serve you in future business.
  我们希望能在将来的业务中为您提供服务。

（2）拒绝。

① 对给对方带来的不便表示歉意。

- We very much regret that…
  我们感到很遗憾……

② 解释原因并表明自己的立场。

- After a check-up we found that…
  检查后我们发现……
- We are of the opinion that…
  我们的意见是……

③ 直接拒绝或建议可能的解决办法。
- As this is due to the mistake of the carrier, we hope you will refer it to…
  由于这是船运公司的失误造成的,我们希望您与……联系。
- We regret being unable to accept your suggestion to…
  我们很遗憾不能接受你方……的建议。

④ 希望继续与对方合作。
- We hope this will not affect our friendly relationship.
  我们希望这不会影响我们的友好关系。

必备词汇和句型

1. on arrival of… 在……到达之后
2. replacement goods 替换品
3. cannot but 只得
4. short delivery 短量;少装
5. short weight 短重;货不够秤
6. inferior [ɪnˈfɪərɪə] quality 质量低劣
7. improper [ɪmˈprɒpə] packing 不适当的包装
8. A is attributable to B A 由 B 引起
9. the time limit for claim 索赔期限
   within…days after arrival of the goods 货物到达后……天内
10. go into the matter 调查此事
11. inspection [ɪnˈspekʃən] fees = survey charges 检验费
12. apology [əˈpɒlədʒɪ] n. 歉意,愧疚
    apologize [əˈpɒlədʒaɪz] v. 道歉
    He made a public apology for the company's performance.
    他为公司的表现公开道歉。
    He apologized for being late.
    他为迟到而道歉。
13. claim for trade dispute [dɪˈspjuːt] 贸易纠纷(引起的)索赔
14. consideration n. 研究,关注,思考
    We've given your claim our careful consideration.
    我们已就你们提出的索赔做了仔细研究。
15. investigation [ɪnˌvestɪˈgeɪʃn] n. 调查
    We have already made a careful investigation of the case.
    我们已经对这个索赔案件做了详细的调查。
16. inability [ɪnəˈbɪlɪtɪ] n. 无能力
    We regret our inability to accommodate your claim (= We are not in a position to entertain your claim).

UNIT 8

很抱歉我们不能接受你方索赔。

17. incorrect [ˌɪnkəˈrekt] *adj.* 不正确的,不合格的
    Claims for incorrect material must be made within 60 days after arrival of the goods.
    有关不合格材料的索赔问题必须在货到后60天内予以解决。

18. survey report   检验报告

19. claim [kleɪm] *v.* 索赔,要求 *n.* 赔偿,赔偿金
    claim 的相关词：
    claimant [ˈkleɪmənt]   索赔人
    claimee [kleɪmˈiː]   理赔人(被索赔人)
    claims settlement   理赔
    claims assessor [əˈsesə]   估损人
    claims settling agent [ˈeɪdʒənt]   理赔代理人
    claim letter   索赔书
    claims documents   索赔证件
    claims statement   索赔清单
    claims rejected   拒赔
    lodge/make/register/file/raise a (one's) claim with/against/on sb.
    向某方提出索赔
    We are now lodging a claim with you.
    我们现在向贵方提出索赔。
    We filed a claim with (against) you for the short weight.
    关于短重问题,我们已向你方提出索赔。
    The buyer raised a claim against the carrier.
    买方向承运人提出索赔。
    settle a claim = be in settlement of a claim   解决索赔
    We have received your remittance in settlement of our claim.
    我们已经收到你方解决我们索赔问题的汇款。
    entertain/accept a claim   接受理赔
    withdraw/waive a claim   撤销索赔

Part 2   范例及讲解

1. 买方因质量问题提出索赔

范例1：买方提出索赔请求

To：Fred Gao
From：Gary Robinson

Subject：Quality claim

Dear Fred,

We have recently received the **false eyelashes**① which you shipped last month. However, 30% of the false eyelashes were seriously damaged with the packing boxes broken. I am not sure whether these goods were already broken before delivery.

This has brought much **inconvenience**② to us since we has to **postpone**③ our sales. We ask you to **cover**④ our loss which is USD3,000.

I would like to receive 30% of the goods you **reissue**⑤ as soon as possible. Please deliver them by air **at your cost**⑥.

Best wishes,
Gary

【讲解】

① eyelashes　*n.* 睫毛　　false eyelashes　假睫毛

② inconvenience［ˌɪnkən'viːniəns］ *n.* 不便

We regret any inconvenience it may have caused.

我们对可能造成的所有不便深表歉意。

③ postpone［pəʊs'pəʊn］ *v.* 推迟　　postpone = delay

The foreign ministers decided to postpone the meeting.

各国外长决定推迟会议。

④ cover　*v.* 包含,补偿

cover our loss　补偿我们的损失

⑤ reissue［ˌriː'ɪʃuː］ *v.* 补发

The material will not be reissued if lost.

材料如有丢失,将不予补发。

⑥ at your cost　费用你方承担

We shall insure these goods at your cost.

我方将对货物投保,费用由你方负责。

【译文】

亲爱的弗雷德:

我们最近收到了您上个月寄出的假睫毛。然而,30%的假睫毛因外包装盒破裂而被损坏。我不确定这些货物在交货前是否已经坏了。

> 　　这给我们带来了很多不便,因为我们不得不推迟销售。我们要求您赔偿3000美元的损失。
>
> 　　我们需要尽快收到您补发的30%的货物。请空运发给我们,费用由你方承担。
>
> 加里谨上

范例2:卖方提出合理理由拒绝索赔回复

> To：Gary Robinson
> From：Fred Gao
> Subject：Re：Quality claim
>
> Dear Gary,
>
> 　　We regret to **note**① your complaint **respecting**② the eyelashes we sent to you last month.
>
> 　　We have already made a careful **investigation**③ of the case and find the goods **in question**④ were in **first-class**⑤ condition when they left here, **as was evidenced by**⑥ the **clean B/L**⑦. Therefore, the damage must have taken place **in transit**⑧. We are **apparently**⑨ not liable for the damage and would advise you to claim against the shipping company who should **hold responsible**⑩.
>
> 　　Anyway, we thank you for bringing this to our attention. If needed, we shall be pleased to **take the matter up**⑪ **on your behalf**⑫ with the shipping company concerned.
>
> Your faithfully,
> Gao

【讲解】

① note　*v.* 留意,了解　　note = learn

② respect　*v.* 关于　*n.* 尊重　　respecting = regarding

③ investigation　*n.* 调查
make a careful investigation of sth.　仔细调查某事

④ in question　涉及的,所说的,存在问题的
The player in question is Jack.
我们所说的那个选手是杰克。

90

⑤ first-class *adj.* 最好的,一流的

⑥ as is evidenced by 通过……可证实

⑦ B/L=Bill of Lading *n.* 海运提单

clean B/L 清洁海运提单   unclean B/L 不清洁海运提单

海运提单由船运公司签发,若货物无破损等问题,船运公司会签发清洁提单;若货物或包装等存在破损状况,船运公司会签发不清洁提单。这里船运公司签发了清洁提单,说明卖方装运时货物完好。

⑧ transit ['trænsɪt] *n.& v.* 运输,经过

in transit 运输途中

During their talks, the two presidents discussed the transit of goods between the two countries.

会谈中,两位总统讨论了两国间货物运输的问题。

⑨ apparently [ə'pærəntli] *adv.* 很明显地,看来

⑩ hold responsible=be held responsible 承担责任

⑪ take the matter up 处理此事

I intend to take the matter up with the management.

我想和管理层讨论这个问题。

⑫ on your behalf 代表您

【译文】

> 亲爱的加里:
> 　　我们很遗憾地看到您对上月寄给您的假睫毛提出投诉。
> 　　我们已经对此事进行了仔细的调查,发现涉及的货物在离开这里时完好无损,正如清洁提单上所证明的那样。因此,损坏一定发生在运输途中。我们对损坏不予负责,并建议您向应该承担责任的船运公司索赔。
> 　　不管怎样,我们感谢您告知我们这件事。如有需要,我们将很高兴代表您向相关的船运公司提出此事。
>
> 　　　　　　　　　　　　　　　　　　　　　　　　　　　　　　　　　高谨上

2. 买方因短量提出索赔

范例1:买方提出索赔请求

> To: Jim Fang
> From: Louis Scott
> Subject: Short delivery claim

Dear Jim,

Thanks for your **prompt**① shipment of our order No.117. We regret having to inform you that **upon**② checking, we found a **short delivery**③ of 150kg which can be evidenced by the **survey report**④ enclosed.

As the **sales season**⑤ is coming very soon, please send us the **short-delivered**⑥ goods without delay. At the same time please accept our claim against you for our loss **amounting to**⑦ USD2,000 plus the **inspection fee**⑧.

Thanks you in advance for your cooperation.

Best regards,
Louis

【讲解】

① prompt   *adj.* 迅速地
prompt shipment   迅速地装运
② upon   *prep.* 基于……,在……之上   upon = on
upon checking   当检查时
③ short delivery   短量,少装
a short delivery of 150kg = 150kg is short delivered   少装了150千克
④ survey report   调查报告
⑤ sales season   销售旺季
⑥ short-delivered = short-shipped   短量的,少装的
⑦ amount to   总计
⑧ inspection fee   检查费

【译文】

亲爱的吉姆:
　　感谢您对我们第117号订单及时发货。但我们很遗憾地告诉您,经过检查,我们发现您少装了150千克的货,附上的调查报告可以证明这一点。
　　由于销售旺季即将来临,请立即将少装的货发给我们。同时请接受我方向您索赔2000美元及检验费。
　　提前感谢您的合作。

最好的问候
路易斯

范例2：卖方道歉并理赔回复

To：Louis Scott
From：Jim Fang
Subject：Short delivery apology

Dear Louis,

We learned with great regret that the shipment was 150kg short delivered. We immediately went into the matter and found that the short delivery was **due to**① an error **on the part of**② our packing staff. We **apologize**③!

Now we have arranged for the right goods to be delivered to you at once. Relevant document will also be mailed to you as soon as they are prepared.

I know it has brought you a lot of trouble. **Per**④ checking with our boss, we will give you USD2,000 plus the inspection fee to make up your loss.

Our apologies for the inconvenience again.

Yours faithfully,
Jim

【讲解】

① due to   由于
② on the part of   在……一边，由……所作出的，就……而言
③ apologize [əˈpɒlədʒaɪz]   *v.* 道歉
apologize for sth.   为……道歉
apology   *n.* 歉意，愧疚
He apologized to the people who had been affected.
他向受到影响的人道歉。
④ per   *prep.* 按照，根据

【译文】

亲爱的路易斯：
　　我们遗憾地获悉这批货少装了150千克。我们立即调查了此事，发现这次少装是由于我们包装人员的失误造成的。我们向您道歉！
　　现在我们已安排将正确数量的货物立即发给您。相关文件准备好也会立即邮寄给您。
　　我知道这给你带来了很多麻烦。经与老板核对后，我们将给你2000美元及

检验费,以弥补你方的损失。
给您带来的不便,我们再次表示歉意。

吉姆谨上

Part 3　实训

1. Translate the following sentences into Chinese.

（1）We are entitled to register a claim for 20% of the invoice value for inferior quality against the exporter.

（2）After looking into the matter, the surveyors find that the damage was caused by rough handling at the dock.

（3）The discrepancy between the goods shipped and the original sample is unacceptable.

（4）To settle your claim, we agree to make a reduction of 20% of the invoice value, which we think can make up your loss.

2. Translate the following sentences into English.

（1）短量是我们此次索赔的原因。

（2）贵方此次索赔的货物在离开装运港时是完好无损的。

（3）我们要求贵方赔偿由于取消订单可能造成的损失。

（4）收到贵方关于所收原料的质量与所期望的质量不符的投诉,我们深表歉意。

3. Write a reply to this claim letter to settle the claim as the buyer requested.

To: Leo Sun
From: Joseph Butler
Subject: Quality claim

Dear Leo,

　　We have received our order No.336 for stainless steel pans last week. We have examined the shipment carefully and, to our great disappointment, find that they are not of the quality we ordered.

　　The materials do not match the samples you sent us. The quality of some of them is so poor. We have no choice but to ask you to take the materials back and replace them with materials of the quality we ordered.

　　Besides, we must file a claim amounting to USD1,000 plus inspection fee for our loss.

  We look forward to your early reply.

Yours sincerely,
Joseph

【译文】

亲爱的利奥：
  我们上周收到了第336号不锈钢锅的订单。经查验后发现货物质量与商定的质量不相符，本公司非常失望。
  该批货物与样本相差甚远，部分质量极差，我们要求退货并换回与合同要求质量相同的货品。
  另外，我们必须提出索赔，索赔额为1000美元及检验费，以弥补我们的损失。
  请早日回复。

约瑟夫谨上

【答案】

1. Translate the following sentences into Chinese.
（1）我们有权以产品劣质为由向出口商索赔，索赔金额是发票金额的20%。
（2）检验员在深入调查后认定，此次货损是由码头方面的野蛮装卸造成的。
（3）运来的货物与当初的样品不符，我方不能接受。
（4）作为理赔，我们同意少收相当于发票金额20%的货款。我们认为这可以补偿你们的损失。

2. Translate the following sentences into English.
（1）Short weight is what the claim is for.
（2）The goods you are claiming damaged were in perfect condition when they left the loading port.
（3）We ask you to cover any loss which might be caused by the cancellation of the order.
（4）We were very sorry to receive your complaint that the material you received was not of the quality expected.

3. Write a reply to this claim letter to settle the claim as the buyer requested.

To: Joseph Butler

From: Leo Sun

Subject: Quality claim apology

Dear Joseph,

We are sorry to hear of the poor quality of the stainless steel pans we sent to you. We immediately went into this matter and found that this error is due to an error on the part of one of our suppliers who gave us the second-class stainless steel pans this time. We apologize!

Now we have arranged for the high-quality goods to be delivered to you at once.

I know it has brought you a lot of trouble. We will give you USD1,000 plus the inspection fee to make up your loss.

Our apologies for the inconvenience.

Yours faithfully,

Leo

【译文】

亲爱的约瑟夫：

得知我们寄给你方的不锈钢锅质量不好，我们深感遗憾。我们立即着手调查此事并发现，这次我们的一个供应商给我们的是二等不锈钢锅。我们向您道歉！

现在我们已经安排好立刻把高质量的货物发给您。

我知道这给您带来了很多麻烦。我们将给您 1000 美元及检验费，以弥补你方的损失。

对于给您带来的不便，我们深表歉意。

利奥谨上

参 考 文 献

[1] 刘溪. 外贸英语函电[M]. 北京：清华大学出版社，2015.
[2] 杨伶俐. 外贸英语函电[M]. 2版. 北京：对外经济贸易大学出版社，2015.
[3] 陈文汉. 外贸英语函电[M]. 北京：中国人民大学出版社，2013.
[4] 伊辉春. 新编外贸英语函电[M]. 北京：化学工业出版社，2016.
[5] 兰天. 外贸英语函电[M]. 7版. 大连：东北财经大学出版社，2015.
[6] 傅龙海. 外贸英语函电实务精讲[M]. 北京：中国海关出版社，2013.
[7] 程同春，程欣. 新编国际商务英语函电（修订版）[M]. 南京：东南大学出版社，2013.
[8] 陈振东. 新编外贸英语函电写作教程[M]. 北京：对外经济贸易大学出版社，2010.
[9] 董晓波. 国际贸易英语函电[M]. 北京：北京交通大学出版社，2010.

图书资源支持

感谢您一直以来对清华版图书的支持和爱护。为了配合本书的使用，本书提供配套的资源，有需求的读者请扫描下方的"书圈"微信公众号二维码，在图书专区下载，也可以拨打电话或发送电子邮件咨询。

如果您在使用本书的过程中遇到了什么问题，或者有相关图书出版计划，也请您发邮件告诉我们，以便我们更好地为您服务。

我们的联系方式：

地　　址：北京市海淀区双清路学研大厦 A 座 701

邮　　编：100084

电　　话：010-83470236　010-83470237

资源下载：http://www.tup.com.cn

客服邮箱：2301891038@qq.com

QQ：2301891038（请写明您的单位和姓名）

书　圈

扫一扫，获取最新目录

课　程　直　播

用微信扫一扫右边的二维码，即可关注清华大学出版社公众号"书圈"。